Farming in a Nutshell~~shell~~house

Farming in a Nutshell

house (Nutshell with "shell" crossed out and "house" written over)

Aeneas Precht

Western Producer Prairie Books
Saskatoon, Saskatchewan

Cover and interior illustrations and design by Warren Clark
Printed and bound in Canada

The publisher acknowledges the support received for this
publication from the Canada Council.

Western Producer Prairie Books is a unique publishing
venture located in the middle of western Canada and owned
by a group of prairie farmers who are members of
Saskatchewan Wheat Pool. From the first book in 1954, a
reprint of a serial originally carried in the weekly newspaper,
The Western Producer, to the book before you now, the
tradition of providing enjoyable and informative reading for
all Canadians is continued.

Canadian Cataloguing in Publication Data

Precht, Aeneas, 1947–

Farming in a Nutshellhouse

ISBN 0–88833–328–5

1. Farm life - Canada - Humor.   2. Farmers - Humor.
I. Title.

PN6178.C3P74 1991   C814'.54   C90–097202–5

This book is dedicated to my parents with love.

My main claim to fame as their son was that in retrospect, I made the Dirty Thirties seem not so bad to them.

(Putting up with the Great Depression was nothing compared to putting up with my little depressions.)

Contents

CONTENTS

Farming **house**
in a Nuts~~hell~~

one

Farming Facts

Farmers practise the second oldest occupation in order to feed themselves. This practice is called farming. This makes farmers second-class citizens.

All others are first-class citizens. As such, they practise the oldest occupation on farmers in order to feed themselves. This practice is called business.

In today's world, to go second class is to ride at the back of the bus. Unfortunately, farmers don't own buses. They only have pickup trucks. So farmers have to ride in the back of the truck and choke on dust. This makes farmers slightly less than second-class citizens. This is one difference between the theory and practice of farming.

There are many differences between the theory and practice of farming—many verses to the chorus of the farmer's lament, "My grain is a headache."

two

What Farming Is Like

Life is just a convenient way of putting in time until we die. The truth is, life seems to go nowhere most of the time.

One of the things that makes life tolerable is pretending there is a point to it all. Pretending there are rules and as a consequence, that it's possible to win at life. This is why many people treat life as a game with winners and losers.

Farmers also think of farming as a game with winners and losers. Unfortunately, the losers are nearly always the farmers. To demonstrate how this can be, I've invented a game called **Farmer**.

The basic idea of the game of **Farmer** is simple. The first player to go broke wins a regular job, a house in the city, and everlasting peace. The game itself uses several dodeca-hedrons, or twelve-sided dice, with each die labelled variously as time, machinery, money, weather, bank, and so on. There are a number of drawcards, and the board is held together with baling wire so as to create the ambience of a farm.

Although the idea is to go broke and head for the bright

lights of the city, the game is constructed so that, like the donkey and the carrot, that tantalizing goal is always slightly out of reach.

The board is four-sided, representing the four seasons. Each player begins with a mortgage on eight quarter sections of land, ten broken-down pieces of farm equipment, and a $50,000 operating loan.

In spring, for instance, dice rolling may produce a sequence of instructions something like the following: "Begin seeding, tractor breaks down. Spend $2,000 for repairs and wait four days. Rain sets in for two weeks."

A typical roll on the summer side of farming might contain something like "Forfeit vacation. Grasshoppers have eaten tent." or "Player's income tax returns are audited. Pay $5,000."

Harvest time. The following scenario could represent an average roll for the game of **Farmer**. "Delayed harvest. Suffer 24 percent loss of yield. Speculation of bumper crop for next year depresses grain prices."

And for those financial hotshots who see an easy dash to the finish line by way of bankruptcy—sorry, it won't work. Rule number 74 of **Farmer** states: "The grand prize of life in the city is based on the ability to borrow money. Bankrupt farmers cannot borrow money. Bankruptcy does not constitute a win. Player is assessed a 10 percent penalty on all assets for trying to cheat."

And even when that exciting point of abject poverty is reached (wherein it finally becomes possible to sell off land and machinery so as to pay back the bank), it isn't so easy to win. Rule number 155 states: "To win grand prize, player must retain, after liquidation, enough cash for a down payment on a house in the city. Failure to do so means player must negotiate with the bank to mortgage eight quarter sections of land, buy ten broken-down pieces of farm equipment, and borrow $50,000 for an operating loan so as to continue farming."

Anyway, that's how farming, and the game of **Farmer**, are played. So why would anyone want to farm?

3

◀ three ▶

Why Farmers Farm

Needless to say, there won't be many winners in my game of **Farmer**. This is because the game is deceptive, about as deceptive as trying to win at the real-life game of farming. So why do farmers continue to farm if they can't win at farming? It's all rather complicated, and it goes like this . . .

The economics of present-day farming have driven the "also-rans" from the land. Consequently, the only remaining farmers are successful farmers. It therefore follows that all successful farmers must also be good businesspeople to have survived in farming this long. Now, businesspeople operate businesses to make money. Since farms don't make money, good businesspeople (i.e., successful farmers) would never invest money in farming.

So. We've established that all existing farmers are success-ful farmers, and that all successful farmers are also good businesspeople. And we know that all good businesspeo-ple won't touch farming with a 3.048006-metre pole.

By implication, all good farmers must want out of farming. So how come there are still good farmers farming?

4

Catch 22. Farms are very expensive things. Successful farmers can only sell their farms to other successful farmers (or other successful businesspeople). However, because farms are such a poor investment financially, successful people won't touch them.

The only other people who might want to buy a farm are nonfarmers who want to become farmers. And because of today's high cost of farms and farming, any others who may want to buy a farm have to borrow the money.

Banks have a lot of money. However, bankers are good businesspeople. They won't lend money to poor businesspeople or for poor business investments. So banks won't lend money to anyone who wants to buy a farm because in wanting to buy a farm a person is demonstrating he or she is a poor businessperson and hence undeserving of a bank loan.

In short, farmers farm because farmers can't get out of farming.

Eventually this drives farmers mad. Hence the refrain of the farmer's lament, "My grain is a headache."

By the way, does anybody out there want to buy my farm? Cash of course.

◀ four ▶

Notes on Rebecoming a Farmer

It turns out that getting back *into* farming is just as difficult as getting *out* of farming. I returned to the land after a number of happy years bumming around Canada working at enough jobs to put me into the *Guiness Book of Employables*.

Unfortunately, all good things must come to an end. Youth for example. At twenty-five, like every other twenty-five-year-old, I was immortal. Then I hit thirty. I've often thought that maturity must be a virus. Nearly everyone catches it, and like herpes, nobody ever gets rid of it. And short of death, there isn't any apparent cure for growing up.

So I did what so many farm boys have done after leaving home and vowing never to come back. I came back. I was seduced by what I wanted farming to be.

Being a bit of a Utopian, I had been continually searching for eternal happiness during my travels. Age and a short memory convinced me such happiness could be found by

6

going back to the land. Being a farm boy, I knew that avoiding Murphy and his in-laws and the inevitable frustrations of farming was impossible. However, I resolved to avoid dwelling on the unpleasant by utilizing the Buddha's approach—the perfect smile toward friend, foe, or frustration. (Even Buddha spent some time studying various disciplines of knowledge.)

So the first thing I did when I returned to the farm was call up the Dane Carnegie School of Magic, Illusion, and Speed Welding and enrol in a course specifically designed for farmers.

The instructors put me through their toughest farming-readiness course. First they tied me to a chair and made me watch a short film documentary over and over for nine hours. It was one of those Hinterland "Who's Who" things that's shown on television. You know, the ones that go "Ta-da-dada. . . . The gopher is a cute and cuddly rodent loved by all on the prairies. . . . Ta-da-dada."

Then I was locked in a tractor cab filled with a swarm of flea beetles, a day-glo centrefold of the Federal Agriculture Minister, and a tape recording of Department of Agriculture farming advice designed to repeat itself with endless variations. I remember thinking when I emerged from the cab some three weeks later that now I could look on any situation and laugh.

It worked for a while. Regardless of what went wrong, I laughed it off. At that point all my farmer friends noticed my unnatural behaviour and started avoiding me like the plague. Murphy struck, "Any farmer who can laugh at misfortune is either nuts or he isn't a farmer."

And since farmers can farm alone only as long as farmers never have to shovel out a granary alone, Murphy's last law came into effect, "You can't escape Murphy." Upon rediscovering that I couldn't avoid Murphy, I vowed to leave the farm and never come back.

◀ five ▶

So Then What?

The day a farmer packs in farming is the day a farmer starts packing lunches for the office. No big deal. Work is work, right?

Wrong. The thought of going back to all those horns, hustlers, and high-rises made me cringe. I realized I wasn't mentally prepared for another shot at city life, so I decided to do a little practice city living while still on the old homestead.

To do that, I built an apartment simulator. I pitched my tent two feet from the dingiest wall of my shop, and wired it with a background tape recording of loud footsteps, arguments, and toilet flushes (all for the sake of ambience of course).

To complete the simulation, I installed triple-deadbolt locks, wire gratings over the window panels, and a burglar alarm. I even hooked up an answering machine to my computer so as to be able to stay in touch with my doorbell, thermostat, coffee maker, broker, and John Lennon record collection.

8

I moved in a mountain of canned food, and two of those cheap chromed can openers that adorn supermarket shelves like poor relatives at the reading of a rich uncle's will.

Things began badly. The first opener I used was the type that gets clamped on the lid, allowing the cutter to rotate around the can top. At the first contact with metal, the cutter slipped off like a drunk from a temperance meeting. No problem, says I. Being the cautious lad I am, I pulled out my reserve, one of those old standbys that looks like a one-pronged trident discarded by Neptune. With my best karate yell, I impaled the can and proceeded to twist, pump, and hack my way around the edge in a decreasing spiral that left a hole in the top large enough to get at least five beans out at one try. Enough is enough I thought, and headed for my shop. That's when I discovered that I was, somehow, locked in my tent.

Well, to make a long story short, one of my neighbours finally heard my yells and eventually some firefighters and their jaws of life arrived to rescue me from my tent. They also reopened my beans.

By way of reflection I realized that if this was an omen, life in the city was probably going to be just as tough as life on the farm.

I opted to stay on the back 40.

I have only two unanswered questions in all this. First, when does one learn that the grass isn't greener on the other side?

Second, does anybody out there want to buy my farm?

◀ six ▶

Real Farmers Like to Gamble

I quit farming at least once in any given year. However, because farm land is such a terrible investment, nobody will buy me out. Therefore I also take up farming at least once in any given year.

Shortly after I returned to farming I discovered that the other thing I had to take up at least once a year was debt. Farmers refer to this as **Lottofarm**. The comparison of farming to a lottery isn't accidental.

At first sight lotteries and farms would seem, like apples and oranges, fruit of a different flavour. But the truth is, they're like sugar and aspartame—more alike than different.

Both a lottery and farming offer jackpots. Both have the odds stacked against them. Both look deceptively easy to win at. (For a lottery all you have to do is pick a few numbers to win. For farming all you have to do is plant a few seeds to reap that big harvest.) And both have all manner of experts telling you how to win. (And in both cases, it's the experts who consistently take home any cash.)

There are other similarities. In a lottery, for instance, it's necessary to buy a ticket before having a shot at the prize money. Similarly in farming, it's necessary to invest money at seeding time so as to possibly reap a bumper crop.[1]

This is apples equal oranges in theory.

What about in practice? Again consider the similarities. Lotto players combine horoscopes, fortunetellers, computers, astrologers, and the phone numbers of rich relatives in their quest to find the winning numbers to open Ali Baba's cave.

Farmers follow a similar song and dance by consulting almanacs, the grain futures market, various magical combinations of extinct bank account numbers, factorial combinations of the amounts and locations of local rainfall, along with the soliloquies of soothsayers studying the entrails of present prime ministers, presidents, and premiers. All of which are combined and analyzed at coffee row. For instance . . .

"What'ya plantin' this year?"

"Wheat."

"Yep, wheat's good as any. Price is goin' down though."

"Don't say. Goin' down much?"

"Enough."

"Maybe I'll plant rape."[2]

"Flea beetles is supposed to be bad this year."

"That so?"

"Yup. Feller from the university said so."

"Hmmm. Flax is O.K."

"Straw's hard to get rid of though."

"True enough. Could try barley?"

"Awful itchy."

"Guess I'll grow wheat then."

"Yep, wheat's good as any."

Then having selected a winning combination of crops, they place their bets and buy their tickets. And just how

---

1. This allows a farmer to continue paying on the prize-winning farm the banker allows him to play on as a peon.
2. Real farmers still call rape, *rape* and not *canola*.

does a farmer buy a ticket to win at farming? Simple. He heads into town and drops in on the local banker so as to borrow the price of a ticket for the game of . . . **Lottofarm**.

Lottofarm is that exciting age-old gamble where a farmer plants the banker's $50,000 in the spring, works all summer, and then harvests $50,000 worth of grain in the fall for the banker.

This is *apples equal oranges* in practice.

Which brings up the only instance where lotteries and **Lottofarm** differ. There are many instances where the apparent good fortune of a lottery win has in fact led to the winner's misfortune: lost friends, lost family, and lost fortune — and that's the good news. If such hard-luck lottery winners had lost their tickets, they would never have had to suffer the frustration of taking a bite out of paradise at breakfast and coming up hungry by teatime.

On the other hand, if I should be so lucky as to lose my ticket, I'd still win at **Lottofarm** — the banker always keeps a copy.

Have you ever noticed how apples and oranges can on occasion be indistinguishable from lemons?

seven

Don't Bank
on Farming Profits

Banks like money more than they like farmers.

If it weren't for the fact that farmers earn more money for banks than for themselves, bankers would have nothing to do with us.

Farmers are third world folks in the banking world. Strangely enough, the third world offers a clue to farmers for dealing with banks. A few years back some third world countries formed a debtors' league when they discovered they couldn't repay their loans to the Western world. Their debts were so large that the debtor nations found they could control the amount and time of repayment (if indeed they wanted to repay at all).

That's the point isn't it? If I owe the bank $1,000, I have a problem. If I owe the bank $1,000,000, the bank has a problem. In the case of the third world countries, it's now the banks who have the problem. It's now the banks

13

who do the bowing and scraping.

There's a parallel here to farming. A lot of farmers are in debt. Brazil et al have shown us the solution to money problems: throw the problems back at the banks.

And here's how to do it. Organize a farm debtors' movement. We'll have to call it something nice and snappy like Farmers and Other Debtors Determined to Escape Ripoffs (FODDER for short).

I'm sure such a movement would be wildly successful, mainly because it wouldn't have to do anything: just imitate the third world countries—borrow. First, we FODDERites would have to dig ourselves deeper into debt—easily accomplished by continuing to farm. Then we'd tell the banks we can't pay off said debt. At that point we farmers will finally find our place in the financial sun. And as with the debtors' league of third world nations, the banks will be forced to come bowing and scraping at our doors.

Now I realize there are those who won't have anything to do with FODDER—those who consider a bank loan to be an honourable debt; those to whom money is the basis of world finance; those who think that if everyone pretended money was just paper the world economy would collapse. In short, those content to be fodder.

Well, money *is* just paper. Whatever honour was originally attached to money has since been swallowed up by a world of finance which resembles the set of a Monty Python movie.

Consider. The ubiquitous *they* tell us that every country in the world is in debt. They also tell us that nearly every person in every country in the world is in debt. And to whom do all of us owe this money? That they don't tell us.

Those who are in debt (which is most of the world) can't be the loan sharks. It can't be the banks we owe money to on such a large scale. Banks don't actually have money. They just rent the stuff. Big business isn't the owner. Things are so bad for big business that without government handouts they'd be in soup lines too. Government debt is now totally out of sight. And the commies don't count because they don't have any money, and they don't have anything worth repossessing. There isn't anybody else. The inescapable conclusion is that we owe all our money to nobody and nothing.

Can you believe it? Not even Monty Python's money-making movie moguls of madness have the imagination to invent a world which would sell itself to itself for so much that it couldn't afford itself. Then in an attempt to afford itself, it would finance itself from no one or nothing to the point where it would be unable to repay itself.

It's certainly more than I can explain. It's tempting to label this reality a conspiracy. But that doesn't wash for two reasons. First, there are bound to be some who'd figure their slice of the pie wasn't big enough, so they'd blow the whistle on the others. Greed is like that. The other reason is that I can't imagine someone or a group of someones pulling off a sting of this magnitude without bragging about it. Human nature is like that. So the conspiracy angle is out.

How about human error? Maybe it's all a colossal accounting blunder, a misplaced decimal point or something? But even if some accountant made a mistake, then the accountant auditing the accountant's accounts would find it. So this can't be an error.

The only other possibility is that this is a replay of that old story "The Emperor's New Clothes," where once again we have all become victims of perpetual mention. The debt exists only because we're told it exists and only dummies doubt it.

Belonging to FODDER isn't copping out. It's coping with reality. The third world countries found this out when they gave world finance the raspberry. Debt is in the eyes of the beholder. The third world called the bluff and now it's the Western world that's left holding a bad loan for zillions of dollars that no one really seems to own.

Farmers can do the same thing. They can decide whether they're fodder for the banks or whether they'd rather be FODDER away from the banks.

Figure 1: BALING WIRE
As detailed in chapter twenty-one, "The Theory and Practice of Farming."

‹ eight ›

Chicken Fodder,
(See "Working for")

Most North Americans assume food is overpriced. When consumers complain about the high price of food, they are in fact objecting to being gouged by farmers.

"How the hell can they charge that much for potatoes? They grow them for free!"[1]

It's assumed that farmers grow their food for free. This assumption has led to an erroneous idea of what a farmer is. Most people think of farmers as people who live for free off the land. They think of farmers as kind, self-sufficient, hardworking types whose real reward in life is the day's effort. Most farmers would agree with this assessment. They too think they're idiots for working for nothing.

Farmers work for nothing in the belief that once in a while

---

1. Translation: selling price minus the cost of production (no cost) = infinite profit = gouging.

they'll make enough money to enable them to work a few more years for nothing.

I've just discovered that the reason farmers continue to work for nothing is because of superstitious behaviour.

I've never paid that much attention to superstition. I've always believed it was bad luck to do so. But the other day I had one of those rare moments of cosmic satori[1] whilst browsing the latest issue of my *Touchi Feeli* magazine. I suddenly understood the psychological conditioning inherent in farming.

I dived for my old university text on psychology. Sure enough, I was right. The practices of farmers have become riddled with superstitious behaviour over the years.

Superstitious behaviour is far too difficult to define in abstract terms, but it's rather easy to illustrate in practice. Psychology is like that.

If a pigeon or chicken is put in a box and given a food pellet every now and then, it soon develops an extraordinary mixture of movements. It works like this.

Over time, food pellets are dispersed at random. The bird believes its movements just prior to the appearance of the pellet were responsible for the bit of food. So it repeats those movements again in the hope of more food. Only this time nothing happens. The bird is apt to repeat all its movements a few more times in order to coax some food out of the dispenser. If nothing happens, the bird gives up in disgust and wanders away to do something else. Again quite randomly—more food. The bird goes "aha" and repeats every one of its movements prior to the first food pellet, and then adds on all its subsequent movements up to the appearance of the second pellet (again performed in the belief that its movements just prior to the appearance of the pellet were responsible for the bit of food). The bird continues to add all new behaviours onto all old behaviours as long as it gets an occasional bit of food. It doesn't take long for the original and

---

1. The Zen Buddhist equivalent of the Western "aha."

add on steps to result in the most extraordinary behaviour. Such movements are called superstitious behaviour.

When I look back on it, that describes farming.

One year I'd have a crop failure. No problem. Next year I'd move my rotation around and plant a different crop at a different time. And like the bird, I'd get a money pellet in the form of a grain cheque every now and then. That was enough to keep me planting and harvesting different crops year after year. Superstitious behaviour.

Which also explains my unconventional attitude toward fixing machinery. While farming, I always maintained an unshakeable belief that any machine could be fixed with a big hammer. I now know where that idea came from. I distinctly remember one warm June day my first year back on the farm, when I fixed an ailing carburettor on my old pickup by giving it a small tap with a small hammer. With each succeeding breakdown I increased the number and violence of my taps until my clouts had graduated into sledgehammer blows. Superstitious behaviour.

The evil of superstitious behaviour is that it continues long after the food pellets run out. Even when farmers notice that beating up equipment isn't fixing it, they go on *fixing it*. Even when farmers suddenly realize that the *food pellets* have stopped coming in, they still go on farming. "Maybe next year," they say.

Some may argue against this theory. However, to those unbelievers I put this question, "What else but the theory of superstitious behaviour can explain why a farmer is willing to continue working for chicken feed?"

nine

What Computers Are Really Used for on the Farm

Anyone who works for chicken feed doesn't have much of a credit rating. And anyone who doesn't have much of a credit rating doesn't get much credit from banks these days. Which means a lot of farmers turn to anyone they can turn to in their efforts to borrow a little money. Farmers have even been known to ask other farmers for money.

The world of flyweight farm financing is tough these days. It used to be that I could tell whether it was a safe bet to lend fellow farmers $10 by the way they treated their dog.

No more. Dogs are a luxury. Fewer and fewer farmers can afford luxuries any more. The only return on keeping a dog is affection (a rather intangible sum on the bottom of a spreadsheet). Since finances dictate that farmers be more concerned with spreadsheets than affection, fewer and fewer farmers are keeping dogs. And if a farmer doesn't have access to a dog, it becomes impossible to tell if a farmer is a dog kicker or a dog petter; impossible to tell if a farmer is a $10 keeper, or a $10 returner.

I had to rack my brains and work out several scenarios on my computer before I came up with a sure-fire way to tell which farmers were good loan risks, and as a consequence, which supplicating sodbusters would return my $10.

Strangely enough, it was the computer itself which gave me the idea.

You see, while dogs may be a luxury, computers aren't.

Computers do all sorts of wonderful things for farmers. Computers project bumper crops and enough surplus cash to enable farmers to go away in the winter so as to fish and play in the water. Computers tell farmers when it is most advantageous to sell that bumper crop so as to have enough cash to go away in the winter and fish and play in the water. And because computers bear no relation to the real world, they are wonderful things to play games on during the winter in place of vacations. Computers are also a tax deduction. Dogs aren't.

That being the case, most farmers have computers. That being the case, it should be possible to ascertain whether a farmer is a $10 keeper or a $10 returner by how he treats his computer.

As a consequence, I spent a lot of time analyzing my fellow farmers. I came up with an exhaustive analysis of the various types of farmer computer users and what the probable fate of my $10 would be.

Star Trekkers   Boldly go where no one has gone before. Distinguishing traits: noted for taking their computers apart. Noted for taking their computers in for repairs . . . assuming they have their pickup back together again.

Analysis: Keep your $10 for computer repairs.

Librarians   (Dewey decimalaters to the in-crowd) Insist on understanding everything from page one to the last paragraph on page 3,425,672 (the usual number of pages in any computer manual), by which time their computer is obsolete and has to be replaced with a new one.

21

Analysis: Keep your $10 as a down payment on a new computer.

Bush Pilots   Plug in, turn on, and go. Characterized by pushing keys at random to see what they do. Noted for software crashes, migraine headaches, and selling their grain at the wrong time.

Analysis: Your $10 goes into the vacation piggy bank to cover grain-price losses. Wave bye-bye to your bill.

Politicians   Practically hold a press conference with all their friends every time they get their computer to do anything. Noted for monopolizing conversation on coffee row. They tend to have large phone bills and friends with unlisted phone numbers.

Analysis: Keep your $10 to pay their phone bills.

Handymen   Use big hammers on their computers to coax proper answers out of it. These farmers always have nicknames for their computers. These farmers always have dented computers. These farmers always get different answers to the same question from their computers. Characterized by dithering, indecision, and as a consequence, being late with their farming operations.

Analysis: Your $10 is kept to pay for custom combining their late-maturing grain.

The use of computers in determining whether to loan anyone money has worked out even better than I had hoped. As you can see, any farmer who owns a computer (which is nearly everyone these days) has serious character flaws. And any farmer with serious character flaws (meaning any farmer with a computer) is a farmer to whom it isn't safe to lend $10.

And to those farmers without computers[1] who want to borrow $10, I ask, "If you don't have a computer, how can I tell whether it's safe to loan you $10?"[2]

---

1. By the way, I loaned $10 to a farmer who not only owned a dog, but didn't kick it. He kept the $10 for dog food.
2. By the way again, I sold this farm applicant screening method to my banker for $10. I asked him if he'd lend me another $10 till Tuesday. He refused on the grounds that anyone who'd even consider loaning a farmer money was demonstrating poor business sense, and hence, undeserving of a loan.

ten

A Farmer's Best Friend

Whoever stated that man's best friend was a dog, wasn't a farmer. Dogs bite, carry off work gloves, chew on boots, and do doo-doo on the lawn. That's what dogs do.[1]

What dogs don't do is carry repairs out to the combine, bus two hundred gallons of fuel back and forth, and wait patiently outside the bar while the farmer has a cold one on a hot day.

Dogs insist on being petted. And while few people care if you kick your pickup in frustration, most people think anyone who kicks a dog is the lowest of the low.

A pickup truck on the other hand carries and ferries; it can be kicked and it doesn't do doo-doo. Dogs are for boys. A pickup is a farmer's best friend.

My best friend's name is Spot. He's an old Mercury half-ton who's been hit in this spot, that spot, and many other spots. Hence the name Spot. Real farmers always name their pickups.

---

1. And a farmer's best friend certainly isn't a computer. They mess up more often than a five-week-old puppy on a new carpet.

Trouble is, it costs a lot to run a vehicle these days. And since I can't get along without Spot, I had a go at making him more economical and cheaper to run. I succeeded beyond my wildest dreams.

It all happened like this. Everyone knows that air drag on a vehicle can account for up to 90 percent of energy requirements while driving at highway speeds.

Being a farm boy, I put my talents together and designed a cowling which cut air drag on Spot by an estimated 30 percent. I figured this should provide a minimum 20 percent in fuel savings. Now since most of the time I'm the only passenger, Spot's engine runs much faster and develops more power than needed, so I put on oversized rear tires and installed a higher ratio rear end, all of which reduced my engine rpm's at highway speed by 27 percent. Even allowing for increased friction, this should mean a good 25 percent increase in fuel economy.

I suppose all the trouble really started when I began to improve the engine efficiency as well. After all, since the price of gas is going to keep going up, investments in fuel efficiency are bound to pay off.

So I added an electronic ignition system that promised to increase my fuel economy by a minimum of 15 percent. I also invested in a set of computer-designed spark plugs which promised a further 12 percent increase in mileage. And to round out the ignition system, I bought a new coil and aviation-type condenser, which together promised to increase my gas mileage another 6 percent.

Well Spot is getting along in years, so I added a set of new super-strong valve springs which promised to reduce my gas guzzling by 10 percent. And I know that the new graphite-based synthetic lubricants I put into the crankcase, transmission, and rear end were bound to save me the advertised 7 percent.

Then I noticed the astounding claims made by a water injector company. Seems this little gizmo injects a controlled amount of water into the manifold to ensure more efficient combustion while saving me 8 percent at the pumps. The company also advocated using an in-throat supercharger which mixes the air and fuel more completely and results in a further 14 percent saving.

At that point I figured that with all this super-efficient combustion I'd better have some way of cleaning out the cylinders rapidly, so I added an exhaust blower which maintains a negative air pressure in the exhaust system. And since it's a well-known fact that back pressure cuts power by at least 12 percent, I figured it was a good investment.

One of the last gimmicks I put on was a gas line pre-heater. This little darling warms gas up to 75° centigrade. Since the prairies are noted more for cold than warmth, I figured that expansion should guarantee that heating four litres of cold gas from the tank would deliver five litres of hot gas at the car. Simple mathematics showed I should save 20 percent.

So how did it all work out? Like I said at the beginning, I succeeded beyond my wildest dreams. I was nearly consumed by success.

After I got everything on and working, I topped up Spot's fuel tank and headed out to the highway. Everything went along fine until I lit up a cigar to celebrate. All I can figure is that Spot became so fuel efficient that he passed the 100 percent mark and started, not using, but making fuel. What with an already full tank . . . well, it must have been the match that set off the explosion.

‹ eleven ›

A Man for All Seasons, or What Is Time to a Farmer?

While a farmer's best friend may be his pickup, his worst enemy is time. Time conspires against farmers. Farmers may not know why, but they do know all isn't right with the round-and-round motions those little arms make on their wrist.

Until Einstein, physicists were convinced that time was one of the gold standards of the universe, one of the immutable measures in a mindless muddle of metric misery. After Einstein, physicists came to understand that wasn't the case. Near the speed of light, time starts to do weird things. Unfortunately, Einstein wasn't a farmer or he could have added another instance when a wristwatch needs to spend some couch time in a psychiatrist's office. As harvest time approaches, weird things happen as well.

Consider. Crops always seem to be ripe before farmers are ready to harvest them. Harvesting always takes twice

26

as long as it should. There is never enough time to do every-thing; conversely, there is always time to do anything twice (such as last fall when I backed into a grain auger because I didn't have time to set guide markers up, at which point I discovered I had lots of time to set guide markers up after I straightened out the grain auger). The list goes on.

I have a theory about why this happens. I'm convinced harvest coincides exactly with the annual passage of a parallel world where time operates in reverse. This sudden passage of another world's reversed time causes our time to fluctu-ate. This sudden interaction with another world's time would explain a lot of the unexplained about harvest.

It would explain why it isn't the farmer's fault for not having his combine ready when the crops are. This passing world causes time to suddenly leap two weeks into the future. Simple logic will demonstrate that it's impossible to be ready today for something that will always be two weeks ahead of you in time.

This also explains why harvesting seems to take twice as long as it should; it's always two weeks later than it other-wise would be.

And why it seems to be impossible to get anything done the longer a harvest takes. The more a farmer goes into the future, the farther he goes into the past; the more he does, the less he gets done.

This reverse time theory explains quite nicely why it is that while there's never enough time to do everything, a farmer can always find enough time to do anything twice.

The reason there's never enough time to do everything, yet always time to do things twice, is complex. To begin with, a farmer is always two weeks behind during harvest time. In an effort to make up that lost time, the farmer hurries and tries to cut corners. Cutting corners causes crunches. A harvest crunch then has to be undone and redone—the doing-it-twice business.

On the surface doing anything twice might seem like a waste of time. Not to a farmer. Because of the peculiarity of the harvest time warp, when everything is going wrong it only seems that time is being lost. Farmers know that the more things go backward, the faster forward time actually goes. Hence once a farmer screws up and backs his or her truck into the grain auger, the farmer begins gaining on that perpetually lost two weeks, and is in actuality, saving time.

In theory this is why all farmers rush around during harvest making mistakes and doing everything twice. They know that in the long run they are gaining a lot of time.

twelve

Watching Time

Man oh man! Where do the years go, eh? Keeping track of the years is simple up to the age of about twenty. After that, time's a blur. Experts tell us you have to associate to remember—which, strangely enough, is exactly how farmers keep track of the years. . . .

"Remember when Ned died?"

"Lemme see, so what year was that?"

"Happened back in '56 as I recollect, cause that was the drought."

"No, no. Emma got hitched in '56 an I remember that cause it was two years after that accident that crippled old John, cause it was the same year I got my new car."

"No, you got your car three years before that accident cause I remember the wife was in the hospital two years before that accident."

"No. I remember your wife was in the hospital during harvest, so it had to be the year before because that was the same year I had Jimmy, and I distinctly remember him having his fourth birthday out in the field during harvest

29

and that was the year of the drought."

"No, cause the drought was the same year the Robbins quit farming and that was only three years after the wife was in the hospital because that was two years after Ned died."

"That's right. So what year was that?"

I couldn't have said it better myself.

The strange thing is, that while farmers can pinpoint past years with pinpoint accuracy, they misplace days in a week.

Who hasn't known a farmer to get the days in a week confused, and heard that same farmer sheepishly explain, "I could'a swore it was Tuesday. Where an'a heck does the week go?"

From this people conclude one of two things. They either assume that because farmers are their own bosses, work their own hours, and consistently misplace a number of days every week, clock time isn't very important on the back 40; or else they assume that farmers don't have enough air in their heads to keep their ears apart.

Which just goes to show how little is really known about farmers. The years are very important to a farmer. Without an accurate accounting of the years, how would farmers know when it's time to retire? And the time of day is very important to a farmer. Without a watch how would a real farmer know when it's time to hit coffee row at the local cafe?

It's the days themselves which get shuffled carelessly by farmers. Every real farmer knows that losing days can be very convenient. If everything isn't done by Sunday, then losing a day midweek gains an extra working day at weekend.

And in Saskatchewan at least, this cavalier attitude to time has a historical basis.

In Saskatchewan the whole problem of misplaced time was reinforced with the resolution of the problem of different time zones. It used to be that asking the time of three different people resulted in three different answers, all of them correct.

It's true. That's the way it used to be in Saskatchewan some years ago. What with the seasonal comings and goings of daylight-saving time, travelling in Saskatchewan used to be like time-tripping. It was possible to arrive somewhere even before leaving home (which is probably another reason why we Saskatchewanians are so flighty).

It was, in short, clock schizophrenia.

As it was a fault of geography, the problem of living with more than one time zone in the same province was considered to be unsolvable. Now it's a fact that the 105th meridian really does split Saskatchewan in two. And historically at least, this was considered a legitimate reason to give Saskatchewan at least two different time zones.

The ending of different time zones in Saskatchewan occurred simultaneously with the introduction of metric measurement. And it happened like this.

Consider that the 100th parallel of longitude lies just outside our eastern border while the 110th parallel runs along our western border—a difference of exactly ten degrees.

And what does the number ten suggest? It suggested itself to me too—metric time. Metric time would take advantage of those natural metric borders. Metric time would deliver Saskatchewanians what had till then been denied them, only one time zone.

No more Saskatchewan days split up by central daylight saving, mountain standard, mountain daylight saving, and "Hockey Night in Canada." No siree, just tens, hundreds, and thousands.

Trouble is, the government folk didn't see it my way. They said they were already having a hard time selling metric measurement and the introduction of metric time would get them thrown out of office. To make a long story short, they promised to do away with the existent two or more time zones if I promised not to tell the newly formed Metric Commission about my idea of metric time to be measured in hours, centiminutes, and milliseconds.

At the time I was kind of disappointed to see my idea swept under the rug. I suppose I should have been elated. After all, I single-handedly forced the doing away with of all those time zones.

Saskatchewan farmers quickly adjusted to this one time zone, to the fact that no longer would they have to adjust to time, that in reality, for the first time, time had adjusted to them. Then the trouble started. Having been given an inch, farmers expected a mile.

Farmers immediately began expecting time to always adjust to them. They began throwing days away. They began throwing weeks away. Then they began missing the arrival of their government cheques in the post office. At that point farmers (at least in Saskatchewan) came to realize that ignoring time wasn't always in their best interests.

thirteen

Mealtime Mania

While farmers may play, bend, ignore, or stretch *real* time, they never mess around with mealtime.

Mealtime is serious time on a farm. City folk may have power lunches till 2:00 in the afternoon, and go out for a fashionable dinner late in the evening. It doesn't work that way on the farm. Down on the back 40 mealtimes are carved in stone. First of all, lunch is something that's taken out to the field at 10:30 in the morning, and 3:00 in the afternoon. Dinner is served at home at exactly 12:00. Supper is served at home at exactly 6:00.[1]

In theory, farmers should be able to eat their meals in under three minutes. This is because three minutes is the average length of time it takes a combine grain hopper to empty itself (at which point the farmer must be back on the combine and ready to begin threshing again).

---

1. Real farmers don't go out to restaurants for dinner or supper unless it's tax deductible.

MEALTIME MANIA

In practice farmers always eat their meals in under three minutes in case they ever grow a crop good enough to actually have to empty the hopper more than once.

fourteen

The Ultimate in Time Control

Except for regularly scheduled meals, farmers play fast and loose with time. Farmers are aware of this fact. So are farm writers. Time management is hot news these days. It seems every farm newspaper and magazine has a scheme for helping me wring a few more minutes out of each day. This is all well and fine for a hypothetical, well-adjusted farmer who can be counted on to look at time and life rationally—a rather irrational attitude from my point of view.

My psychological altitude to time has led me to squander more of the stuff than I've saved—experts notwithstanding. Realizing that there are probably other kindred farming souls out there who are suffering from time trauma, I've devised a solution to all time-management problems on the farm. I've invented the Swiss army watch. This minute manager will do for farmers what the Swiss army knife does for campers, namely: everything.

The Swiss army watch features a time-winder to compress or expand time. For example, if wintertime drags, this watch will automatically assign more of that unwanted time to summer vacation or harvest time. This will tend to even out a farmer's year.

The converter switch changes the shape of the watch. One push and it turns into a Rolex so as to convince the banker that a farmer is doing well enough financially to be worthy of a loan extension. A second push turns the watch into a cheap $1.95 digital for those intimate moments during an audit when you want to give the impression of harmless dotage. In this mode it consistently shows the wrong time and alternately beeps, quits, and restarts for no apparent reason. A third push resets it to normal.

The nag switch is designed to remind a farmer of important things such as taking along a list of needed parts, cheque book, wallet, money, measuring tape, and callipers when going into the city for repairs. It will endlessly nag the farmer to slow down and to not sit in the family car when wearing dirty work clothes.

The auto-message is a handy little extra whose preset program will activate a message to remind the wearer when it's coffee time at the local restaurant, the time of the next hockey game on television, or when a low-pressure area has moved over his favourite fishing hole.

The calendar-calculator function I've built in keeps track of time in a user-friendly fashion. For instance, when it's bank payment time the watch can be set so that it will automatically prove the payment isn't due for another five weeks. This feature is based on the premise that nobody (not even a banker) will question the result of any arithmetic computation done by any electronic device. It's also a useful extra for confrontations with parking-ticket issuers. It provides demonstrable evidence that the farmer was punctual, implying the parking meter ran out five minutes early.

As a final extra, the Swiss army watch can be calibrated to keep track of important farming times such as vacation time and the arrival of various grain and government cheques.

There's only one option I'm still having a bit of trouble

with. That's the installation of a coffee percolator small enough to wear on your wrist, yet large enough to serve a dozen farmers should they inadvertently find themselves grouped at coffee time with no restaurant nearby.

Figure 2: CEREAL GRAINS
As detailed in chapter twenty-one, "The Theory and Practice of Farming."

fifteen

The Other Important Times

Farmers are said to be busy only two times a year—spring (seeding time) and fall (harvest time).

During summertime all farmers do is go to a lake and fish or play in the water.

During wintertime all farmers do is go away on holidays and fish or play in the water.

Imagine how perfect farming would be if this were true.

At which point one must ask—if farming were to become perfect, does that imply farmers would be perfect too?

◀ sixteen ▶

The Farming Goal of Self-Perfection

So how does an average farmer work toward this goal of perfect farming and in doing so, become perfect? By putting the cart before the horse. It goes without saying that if the farmer were to become perfect, he or she would farm perfectly.

So how can the average stubble jumper achieve perfection?

Hard work isn't enough to become a perfect farmer. A perfect farmer has to act like other perfect people.

And in case you haven't noticed, perfect people have hobbies. Supposedly they take up hobbies to relax. In fact, relaxation isn't the reason perfect people take up hobbies. They take up hobbies so as to be perfect. After all, perfect people are well-rounded people. Perfection demands well-roundedness. And in order to prove well-roundedness, it's necessary to take up a hobby.[1]

---

1. Only a perfect farmer can achieve the pinnacle of perfect farming which includes being able to go to a lake so as to fish or play in the water all summer and then going away on holidays so as to fish or play in the water all winter.

It's inescapable. Perfection demands a hobby. So it follows that in their quest for perfection, farmers too must take up a hobby.

Now if you're a slippery sort like myself, you might like to pretend you're perfect without putting in all the effort required. In short, you'll fake it.

So how is the reality of sloth reconciled with the illusion of perfection?[1] As I said, perfection demands a hobby. Similarly, the illusion of perfection demands the illusion of a hobby. How is it possible to take up a hobby while not taking up a hobby?

By taking up a not-hobby.

For all those who enjoy fixing up old machinery, there are an equal number like myself who hate fixing up old machinery. Instead of rushing home and out the door to do chores, I find it more pleasant to not rush home. And when I finally do arrive home after a leisurely drive, I find it even more pleasant to not do chores. Action in inaction—the perfect hobby, (or should I say not-hobby).

So how can these contradictions exist in harmony? Simple. The universe is composed of opposites. For instance, good cannot exist without evil. So it follows that hobbies cannot exist without not-hobbies. And since both are present on the same continuum, who is to say where hobbies end and not-hobbies begin?

For example, some people write books as a hobby. My not-hobby has been not-writing a book describing the virtues of not-hobbies. It's called *Nos, Nots, and Nevers* and the pages are blank. Now consider that because I haven't written it, no one will have to read it, thus saving everyone a lot of time for something more valuable. This book also demonstrates the principle of the not-hobby: how beautiful it is to do nothing and rest afterward.

Questing for perfection isn't as difficult as it first seems.

---

1. Real farmers often pretend they are perfect by spending a lot of time on coffee row telling other farmers how to farm.

And once a perfect farmer, can perfect farming, meaning the freedom to do nothing for the whole year, be far behind?[1]

So what does the average (or perfect) farmer do with all this freedom to do nothing?

Go to a lake and fish or play in the water.

---

1. Since farming implies the freedom to do nothing for most of the year (as anyone from the city knows), then perfect farming implies the perfect freedom to do nothing for the whole year.

seventeen

The Cosmic Balance
of Work and Play

The trouble is, perfect farmers have a conscience. A conscience which reminds them that while they may have all their work done and can therefore go to the lake to fish or play in the water, THERE IS ALWAYS MORE WORK TO DO.

Farmers know this. Being organic types, they are quite attuned to the yin and yang of farming—work and play, the great wheel of life, and all that stuff. They realize that for every force, there is an equal and opposite force. That in order to enjoy play one must work, and that in order to be able to work, one must occasionally play.

All this is true, at least in theory. In practice, farmers have to be convinced they need a holiday before they'll actually go to the lake to fish or play in the water.

Exactly when is it time for a farmer to take a holiday? I know I need a holiday when . . .

1. My brain has all the snap of wet sawdust.

2. I notice that as a result of working longer to get every-thing done, I end up working all the time and getting nothing done.
3. I find myself using a croquet mallet or swinging soap on a rope to swat flies that buzz around my head.
4. I spend more time on alert at night than a Beirut citizen.
5. My attention span can almost manage a commercial without forgetting the message.
6. I don't notice the difference between the commercials and the program.
7. I find Bugs Bunny cartoons terribly relevant.
8. I order the building plans for a forty-foot yacht.
9. I have a hard time remembering words more than four letters long.
10. I have a hard time using anything but four-letter words to describe, criticize, or talk about anything.
11. I'm in too much of a hurry to do things the right way because I have to budget time to do everything twice.
12. I'd rather do the dishes and clean the house than go farming.

When I say yes to more than two of the above, I know I need a holiday. If I score between four and eight, I consider vacationing in a nice rest home. More than eight and I vacation with my psychiatrist.

The flip side of all this is knowing when I've vacationed enough, knowing when I can face phones, fixing, and farming, knowing when it's time for me to get back to work.

I know my holiday should end when . . .

1. I know how many raindrops it takes to form a rivulet.
2. My credit cards are being rejected.
3. I have a hard time using words.
4. I find myself using a croquet mallet or soap on a rope to swat flies that buzz around my head.
5. I find Bugs Bunny cartoons terribly relevant.
6. My brain has all the snap of wet sawdust.

44

If I answer yes to 1 and 2, I know I should get back to the farm. When 3 and 4 also get answered in the affirmative, I know I may not be able to continue farming. When there's a checkmark on all six of the above, nobody at the farm wants me back.

As you can see, my prevacation and postvacation symptoms are startlingly similar. This of course points out the circularity of life and illustrates one of the cosmic lessons of opposites, namely that opposites ain't necessarily so opposite. All of which is quite fortuitous and points out how to use life's little oddities to advantage.

Since it's virtually impossible for anyone to tell if my jitters are caused by excess work or excess play, I can always insist that overwork is to blame. And since opposites balance out in the cosmic scheme of things, I can therefore point out in good conscience that the only cure for overwork is a corresponding amount of overplay.

At that point I can take off some time and go to the lake to fish or play in the water.

◀ eighteen ▶

Let's Go to the Lake

So I went to the lake.

First I tried fishing. In theory, fishing appeals to farmers for a number of reasons.

Farmers don't have to make bank payments for the lake. They also don't have to plant the fish, cultivate the lake, or apply chemicals to make the fish grow. In short, fishing appeals to farmers because as a means of garnering food, it's pure profit. It's free food. And any real farmer has a soft spot in his heart for anything that's free. Yes sir, with fishing it's always harvesting time, payoff time. And unlike grain, which loses value if it stays out too long, fish gain in size and value if they're not caught. The ones not caught today are bigger tomorrow. In theory this is why farmers go fishing: it's free, it's fun, and it's food.

In practice, the reality was somewhat different than I'd expected. My reintroduction to fishing was quite an eye opener. My memories of fishing as a kid included a gentle drive to a nearby lake where, armed with a barbed hook, twenty feet of cotton line, a few minnows, and a few bottles of pop, I caught all the fish I wanted.

No more. Apparently all the stupid fish have been caught. Those left won't fall for that hook-and-minnow business any more. Today's fish are a lot more sophisticated. The truth is that fishing, like farming, has gone hi-tech.

I've come to find out just how out-of-date my free-food theory of fishing really is.

It all began when I went in to buy the barbed hook, twenty feet of line, and a few bottles of beer.[1]

The first thing the salesman asked was what I was planning to catch.

"Fish," I replied.

That response launched him into a half-hour lecture on the habits of pike, walleye, and seventeen shades of trout, along with a few snide lines about my abysmal ignorance of the very serious sport of fishing.

Next day, with my now-superior knowledge and a vast array of the latest in fishing gear, I headed out to meet the boys at the lake.

Many miles later lesson number two began. One doesn't just go fishing.

Allan produced a chart of the lake to match up with the topographical map of the surrounding countryside so as to scale out the probable contours of the lake bottom. Then equipped with this hybrid drawing of the Loch Ness habitat, we set out in the boat to survey the chosen areas with a depth sounder, remote sensing thermometer, a lunar calendar, and a weather forecast for the next week. Compilations of the data (with a laptop computer of course) required the rest of the day.

The projections for fishing the next day indicated the probability of maximum success if we were out and fishing by 0400. We all got up at 0330.

Being half-asleep, I managed to throw my new $150 rod and reel over the side on my first cast. Someone loaned me

---

1. Drinking pop is one of those affectations of youth best left behind.

an extra rod. Not that it mattered. We didn't catch any fish.

The problem, said my wise companions, was simply an insufficient data base. We spent until midnight going over the charts, weather forecast, and depth soundings again. The mistakes found, we retired, until 0330 again.

On my last day I finally managed to catch three very small fish which the guys said was good considering my inexperience, the time of year, having the wrong lures with me, and the fact that fishing had been lousy this month due to temperature inversions set in the Pacific High.

That finished me on the theory of fishing as being free, fun, and food.

But then that's the difference between theory and practice, isn't it? Theories don't have to confront reality. Practice does.

◄ nineteen ►

Magoo at the Helm

So fishing was out. Water-skiing always reminds me of emergency wards. And the lakes are nearly always too cold to swim in. So what the heck is left for a farmer who is supposed to be at the lake playing in the water?

I took up sailing. In theory, sailing is a relaxing way of getting away from the pressures of farming. In practice, it began that way too. It seemed so perfect that I started introducing my friends to the rewards of sailing. Some of my fisher-type farmer friends found it a bit tame though. They said there was no competition, none of the "me or them" attitude they'd come to enjoy with fishing.

"Not so," I exclaimed. "Sailboat racing is as competitive as any other sport." And by way of demonstration I took three of my closest neighbours out in my boat to watch a sailboat race. "You want competition?" I asked them. "Competition you'll get," I told them.

The day we went out was a perfect day for watching a sailboat race. Warm enough to snooze through the dull parts; in deep enough water for my farmer friends to fish

49

through the boring parts; and enough friends on board to converse through the monotonous parts, which in theory takes care of all the important parts of sailboat racing.

There were four of us and our gear aboard my small sailboat that day. It was pretty crowded by the time our lawn chairs and the ghetto blaster were stowed. Ralph was the youngest and the only one to complain. Quite frankly I don't blame him. Since he sat on the cooler and there was no extra room, he had to jump in the lake whenever someone wanted in to get at the beer. Needless to say, that kind of became our joke of the day with Ralph, what with always telling him to go jump in the lake. Needless to say, the crowding made it difficult to sail around the outside of the course so as to be able to watch all the action.

Right about then someone had the bright idea of anchoring near the course so as to watch the race. It seemed like a good idea at the time, even though I had left my anchor on shore in order to stow all our gear aboard. I figured no problem though. Being a farm boy there have been lots of times I've fixed broken machinery out in the field with less of a selection of parts than I had on board that day.

Well it took a few minutes, but I managed to piece together an anchor and anchor line using a pair of pliers tied onto an empty beer can as the anchor, and several strands of fishing line braided together as the anchor line.

We anchored at the edge of the race course. Moments later, Charles, a friend of ours, came by on his sailboard. Being good neighbours, we invited him aboard from his board to my boat for a beer and then tied his sailboard to the end of one of the lines on my sailboat. Charles hadn't even blown the foam off that first beer when the wind piped up a little and my anchor started dragging a lot. Coincidentally, we suddenly noticed that the whole fleet of racers was only about seventy-five metres away and closing fast.

We all sprang into action. Charles jumped back on his

board. Ralph jumped in the lake. I hoisted sail. Suddenly I realized that sinister forces beyond my control had been waiting for this moment all day—that hitherto unrelated forces had been orchestrating events to set me up for this complete fiasco.

That's when I first perceived the Magoo Effect—first realized there was a force beyond Murphy and his in-laws.

In theory, the Magoo Effect is the sudden alliance of unrelated events into a unified disaster. In practice, the Magoo Effect is the malevolent side of whimsy harnessing the forces of darkness.

The recognition of Magoo occurred at the same time I became aware of our predicament. I had gotten my sail up, all the while forgetting that the line tying Charles's sailboard to my sailboat was the line used to adjust my sail. With that line tied on to his board, I couldn't adjust my sail properly. Nonetheless, my boat began sailing away. This caused my line to Charles's sailboard to tighten, preventing Charles from untying the knot to free his craft. And with that line being taut, I couldn't release the wind pressure on my sail and Charles couldn't get his sailboard free. The result was that while my boat couldn't sail very well, it couldn't stop sailing. So boat, board, and boys just sort of sailed backwards and sideways, together.

Then the wind gave a little gust and the anchor started to hydroplane on the surface of the water. Fortunately my boat drifted by the race-marker buoy without snagging it. The anchor wasn't so fortunate. So there we were, boat, board, buoy, and boys drift-sailing sideways, unable to stop or turn. I could see Magoo grinning from the sidelines.

All the racers were in hot pursuit of, and gaining on, the marker buoy which had been snagged by my anchor.

By then the commodore was in his launch and headed our way. I'm not sure if he could see what the problem was, or whether he thought he should just come out and give us a good nautical lecture for being troublemakers.

Anyway someone drove his launch over to us with him standing on the poop deck. As soon as he arrived he began "harumphing" away and telling us to get our confounded scow out of the shipping lanes before the fleet arrived. The racers were gaining on us, no doubt about that. But then so was the shoreline.

The shoreline won. We went aground and everyone started falling into the water. The commodore fell off the poop deck as his launch grounded and he came up sputtering like a marine diesel. Almost immediately the race fleet came tearing up to round that buoy. Soon the whole scene looked like the defeat of the Spanish Armada. There were boats, boards, bottles, bodies, and buoys bobbing, bouncing, and bashing everywhere and everyone. Magoo winked and walked away.

The race committee declared my boat and me a hazard to navigation. The commodore was all for tying me to my anchor and throwing the two of us over the side until somebody on the race committee pointed out we were in less than two feet of water. A second somebody added that disposing of us that way would be littering, punishable by a $50 fine. I pointed out that if they took my beer can/anchor back to the store with me tied to it, they could get a nickel refund on the can. After a lot of discussion they elected to tie my beer can/anchor, albatrosslike, around my neck as a warning to other silly sailors. Then, muttering all, the commodore and his crew headed for the clubhouse to restart the race. One look after them and we headed in the other direction just as fast as we could go. Magoo was strolling down the dock to give the commodore a hand ashore.

Needless to say, none of my farmer friends took up sailing. They pointed out that it was bad enough to farm by Murphy's laws, but they didn't want this Magoo character bugging them on their days off.

If only getting rid of Magoo were so simple.

It appeared that the life of leisure wasn't for me. Suddenly there was nothing for me to do at the lake any more.

That's the difference between the theory of leisure and its practice. The theory promises escape. The practice delivers escapades.

With a heavy heart I returned to my farming.

◀ twenty ▶

Magoo Again

Since that fateful day of sailing, I've often thought that Magoo, and to a lesser degree Murphy, are responsible for the difference between the theory and practice of farming. Magoo is to farmers what Murphy is to the rest of humanity —unavoidable.

Don't misunderstand me, there's nothing wimpy about Murphy. Farmers are the first ones to admit that "whatever can possibly go wrong will." The trouble is, Murphy isn't quite up to the standard of *go-wrongedness* that happens to farmers.

Why? Murphy alludes to a benign force of darkness, where the nature of entropy operates by random chance so as to keep humanity humble. Not so with Magoo. Magoo is malevolent. Magoo has will. And for farming this is an important distinction; things don't just happen to go wrong, things go wrong with a vengeance. Things don't just go wrong at random times, things go wrong at the worst possible moment and in the worst possible place. This is why there is such a difference between the theory and practice of farming.

The recognition of this difference is why all farmers are anthropomorphic, why they think machines are out to get them. Murphy explains that machines will always break down because things will always go wrong. Magoo explains that machines have will: that machines plan when and where to break down.

Murphy promises disorder. Magoo delivers disaster.

What Murphy can't do is explain the timing. Why do things go wrong when they do?

Why do things go wrong at the worst possible time and place so as to cause the most possible damage?

For instance, why will a clutch linkage pin from a combine fall out when a farmer is backing the machine into the shed?

Why doesn't that pin drop off in the field where the rough terrain is more apt to cause a pin to shake loose?

Because a missing clutch linkage pin can't cause any damage in a field. With the whole field to maneuver in, no farmer would have trouble bringing his machine to a stop without incident.

Now consider what happens when that same pin falls out in the close confines of a shed. When the pin falls out, the clutch won't work. With no clutch there's no stopping. And a combine that won't stop backing up continues backing up, right through the shed.

Murphy, after the fact, can't explain why the pin fell out in the shed and not the field, other than to say, "whatever can possibly go wrong will."

No generalities for Magoo. He would predict a priori, that the pin will fall out during close maneuvers because it's the most advantageous place and time to cause maximum disaster.

It's the difference between forecasting rain in June, and forecasting twenty-seven millimetres of rain on June 13th between 0413 and 1744.

Murphy would suggest your combine will break down

"just because." Magoo will predict your combine will break down at that point of land farthest from your shop and your truck, and on a weekend "just because that is the most inconvenient place and time for a breakdown to happen." That's the difference between Murphy and Magoo. It's the peewee leagues versus the pros.

I'm convinced that only Magoo can satisfactorily explain the unexplainable—the difference between the theory and practice of farming.

For instance, what but the Magoo Effect can explain how I once got a medical injury that doesn't exist? It's true. I once had a wrenched nose. Doctor John assured me he had never read about the malady before and that I had the first wrenched nose he had ever seen.

This wrenched nose business all began my second season as a farmer. I had this great crop of mustard sitting out in the field. (Mustard, by the way, is what somebody, somewhere, turns into that yellow stuff used to disguise hot dogs as food.)

In theory all I had to do was get my combine out and harvest the mustard crop. What happened in practice was quite different.

Being fall, I was short of cash. To avoid flattening my wallet even more, I was putting off fixing my combine as long as possible.[1]

Then I panicked and declared harvest officially on.

Day 1   I got my combine, Tweetibird, out of the shed and started checking bearings, belts, and bolts for wear. Then I made up a list of "have to" repair parts and "should" repair parts. The list was long enough to put me into a mild state of shock as well as an advanced state of bankruptcy.

---

1. I've always thought harvest was like writing final exams. There's no sense in studying until panic sets in, because it's only at the moment of panic that total efficiency is achieved. Efforts before that are simply book-pushing. And strangely enough, the onset of panic occurs just in time to get the necessary amount of studying done in order to pass. Ditto for fixing a combine.

Day 2   Shock or not, I went for parts. After finding out the cost of all my repairs, I cut the list in half, knowing full well that my innate ingenuity would enable me to make do for the rest.

On **Days 3**, **4**, and **5**, I got my new repairs onto the combine and jury-rigged the other problem parts just in time for **Day 6** when it began to rain.

I spent **Day 7** on coffee row discussing rain and related combine horror stories, all of which made me realize there were still a lot of questionable parts on Tweetibird. So on that same day I went to the banker to borrow some money to buy the other repairs I should have bought in the first place.

Day 8   I spent all morning sleeping because I hadn't slept the night before because of all the borrowed money I had spent on repairs. In the afternoon, although still somewhat groggy, I began replacing parts on Tweetibird when Magoo stepped in. The wrench that I was pounding on with a hammer slipped and then ricocheted off a sprocket into my face. That broke my nose. I spent the evening bleeding a lot.

Day 9   I went to the doctor and asked if he had anything for a wrenched nose. As I explained before, he was fascinated by my case and pointed out I had just made medical history with an accident thought to be impossible, a wrenched nose.

In the afternoon I took my big hammer to the part responsible for my busted beak. Even today, both my nose and that part still have a decided list to starboard.

By **Day 12** I had most of my combine repairs done which is fortunate because I hate working in the rain, which is just what it did that day.

In theory this all made me feel very old and very vulnerable. Was it a sign of things to come? Was this injury that couldn't happen a sign that my farming days were over, that in practice I just couldn't cut the mustard any more?

Who but Magoo would have planned it? Who but Magoo could have carried it off?

◀ twenty-one ▶

The Theory and
Practice of Farming

I realize that most nonfarmers think I'm making all of this up. Farmers know different. Farmers live with Magoo and Murphy on a daily basis. Farmers live with adversity, the one thing they have learned to count on in a changing world. Such adversity, we are told, builds character. Adversity is the solvent which dissolves farming theory into practice; the forge which sometimes hammers farmers from characters into caricatures.

There are endless farming stories of things that go wrong. Since farming is a solitary pursuit, and since there's a certain amount of jargon in farming, the *go-wrongedness* is generally unobservable or unintelligible to the average (generally unintelligent) observer. In order to correct that oversight, I've compiled the following miniprimer, sort of an *Eh!* of the ABC's of farming terms as they exist in theory and are carried out in practice.

ADJUSTABLE WRENCH
Theory   A wrench designed to fit a number of different-sized bolt heads.

Practice   A wrench which, when pressure is applied, automatically adjusts upwards one size, enabling the wrench to spin freely (see knuckle skinner).

BALING WIRE
Theory   A type of wire originally used to hold hay bales together.

Practice   A type of wire used to hold machines together.

BANKER
Theory   A mild-mannered man who benevolently loans money to farmers.

Practice   A fire-breathing cyclops three metres high known to consume his weight in farmers before breakfast every day.

CEREAL GRAINS
Theory   Plants which farmers grow for sale so as to make money.

Practice   Plants on which farmers spend a lot of money in order to make some money.

COFFEE ROW
Theory   A place where farmers go after they have finished work.

Practice   A place where farmers go instead of working.

COMBINE
Theory   A machine used to harvest grain and designed to separate grain from chaff.

Practice   A machine used during harvest time which separates some grain from the chaff and a lot of money from a farmer.

CUTTING TORCH
Theory   A device utilizing oxygen and a flammable gas to produce a hot flame to cut metal.

Practice   A device which produces a hot flame which cuts (a) into farmers, (b) into any flammable substance, or (c) occasionally into metal. In the event this device is used to cut metal, it nearly always cuts in the wrong place, necessitating the use of an electric welder (see electric welder).

DEFICIENCY PAYMENT

Theory   Money given by governments to farmers to make up the difference between the cost of growing grain and its selling price.

Practice   A deficient government payment.

ELECTRIC WELDER

Theory   An electrical device used to fuse pieces of metal together permanently.

Practice   An electrical device used to fuse (a) two pieces of metal together in the wrong place (see cutting torch), or (b) a farmer to a piece of metal (see doctor).

FARMER

Theory   An individual who makes a profit growing food for others.

Practice   An individual who, in growing food, makes a profit for others.

FENCING

Theory   Parallel wires strung between fence posts and used to keep cattle within the boundary of a field.

Practice   A game played by cattle in which an individual cow, calf, or bull attempts to pass through the fence without breaking the wire. If the wire breaks, the animal loses its turn and returns to the field amid much mooing and other good-natured teasing.

FERTILIZERS

Theory   Growth promoters used to make plants grow.

Practice   The pitch of the salesman selling fertilizer.

GRAIN AUGER
Theory   A device used to convey grain into a granary without manual labour.

Practice   A device which, when it conveys too much grain into a granary, causes a lot of manual labour.

GRAIN TRUCK
Theory   A self-propelled vehicle used to haul grain from the combine to a granary.

Practice   A vehicle which, when it won't start or self-propel, must be hooked behind a tractor in order to haul grain from the combine to the granary.

IMPLEMENT (FARM)
Theory   Any of a general class of expensive machines used in farm work.

Practice   Any of a general class of expensive machines which breaks down when used in farm work. (N.B. In all fairness it must be noted that all farm machines work perfectly during those times in the year when they aren't used.)

JACK-ALL
Theory   A device used to raise a heavy weight.

Practice   A device used to raise a heavy weight high enough to cause excruciating pain when dropped on a foot.

KNUCKLE SKINNER
Theory   The name given an adjustable wrench.

Practice   What an adjustable wrench does to knuckles when used (see adjustable wrench).

OPERATING LOAN
Theory   Money borrowed by a farmer from a bank so as to plant a crop in order to make a profit for the farmer for the year.

Practice   Money borrowed by a farmer from a bank so as to plant a crop and make a profit for the banker for the year.

PARTS a.k.a. **REPAIRS**

Theory   Pieces of metal, plastic, or paper designed to fit specific implements in specific places and kept on hand by machine dealers in the event a farmer has a breakdown and needs repairs.

Practice   Pieces of metal, plastic, or paper which machine dealers are always out of or which never fit specific implements in specific places (see spares).

PICKUP

Theory   What the farmer attempts to do on Saturday night at the local bar.

Practice   The half-ton truck which the farmer takes home on Saturday night instead.

SCREWDRIVER

Theory   A long sharp device used to turn screws into wood or metal.

Practice   What the farmer drinks to ease the pain when the long sharp device slips off the screw and into his hand.

SHOVELLING

Theory   The prehistoric practice of moving grain or cattle manure from one pile to another with a shovel.

Practice   The modern farming practice at coffee row or a tax audit.

SPARES

Theory   Substitute parts which a farmer keeps on hand in order to effect field repairs, such as a spare tire or a spare bearing.

Practice   Substitute parts which, when fitted to the broken machine, turn out not to be so substitute as the salesman indicated.

SWATHER

Theory   A machine used to cut standing grain into a continuous windrow so as to hurry the ripening process of grain.

Practice   A machine which, when it has cut standing grain into a continuous windrow, signals the beginning of the wet season.

TRACTOR
Theory   A device used to pull farm implements in the practice of farming.

Practice   (a) A device used to pull farm implements unless it's too cold out (can't start), or too hot out (shouldn't start), or the air conditioning doesn't work (operator refuses to start), which is most of the time.

(b) In the event the tractor starts and is used to pull a farm implement, it pulls the farm implement apart (such as when hooked to a cultivator which is hooked on a big stone or hooked to a swather which is hooked on a neighbour's fence), necessitating a trip to the city for repairs (see spares, repairs, and parts, and then psychiatrist).

WEEDS
Theory   Wild plants which the farmer tries to kill with expensive chemicals and various fallowing practices.

Practice   Wild plants which grow in abundance in spite of the application of expensive killing chemicals and various fallowing practices.

The object of any primer, of course, is to prepare for future lessons.

And at the end of any primer (of course) is a test. A test which is designed to see if the material has been absorbed. A test which must be passed before going on to advanced studies.

The following test will measure your comprehension of the difference between the theory and practice of farming.

1. Is it true that farmers can, at will, crawl through fields so as to develop a protective black coloration so as to disguise themselves while counting grasshoppers in an attempt to decide whether to spray the pests? Yes or no?

   The answer is "no." Farmers have learned from long experience to send the hired man to crawl through fields so that the hired man can develop the protective black coloration so as to disguise himself while counting grasshoppers in an attempt to decide whether to spray the pests.

2. Farmers are noted for their susceptibility to the common physical disability known as "stressitis nervosa ulceria." This ailment is characterized by
   (a) a short temper
   (b) upset stomach
   (c) inability to sleep

   The answer is (d), all of the above.

3. Farmers treat "stressitis nervosa ulceria" by
   (a) eating too much or not at all
   (b) eating a lot of junk food
   (c) drowning their sorrows in booze
   (d) drinking huge quantities of coffee on coffee row while complaining to other farmers about conditions a, b, and c in question 2
   (e) worrying incessantly
   (f) getting almost no sleep and yelling at everyone in sight

   The answer is none of the above. They go to a lake and fish or play in the water (see chapter 17), or else they get a job in the city (see chapter 5).

4. Farmers listen to morning newscasts because
   (a) they want to make themselves feel better
   (b) misery loves company
   (c) it sets the tone for the day

(d) they are putting in time so as to avoid crawling through fields so as to develop a protective black coloration so as to disguise themselves while counting grasshoppers in an attempt to decide whether to spray the pests until the hired man shows up for breakfast and can be assigned the task

The answer is (d).

5. A farmer pounds on his cultivator when
(a) he is trying to fix it
(b) he stubs his toe walking by it

The answer is no reason in particular, other than it feels good.

6. A modern farmer is in favour of automation because
(a) it will make for more efficient farming
(b) it will make farming operations more economical
(c) he can fire his hired man for refusing to crawl through fields so as to develop a protective black coloration so as to disguise himself while counting grasshoppers in an attempt to decide whether to spray the pests
(d) none of the above

The answer is (d), none of the above. Farmers are in favour of automation because it will reduce their workload, hence allowing them more time to go to a lake and fish or play in the water.

7. Farmers are known to whine and snivel to the government about needing subsidies to combat poor commodity prices, crop failures, and vicious acts of God directed against farmers. They whine and snivel because of
(a) economic necessity
(b) genetic imprinting
(c) family tradition
(d) all of the above

The answer is (d) all of the above, and (e) it works.

If you scored more than ten you are a farmer in which case you should be out working instead of reading this stupid book, stupid.

If you scored more than three but less than ten, you probably are well-acquainted with farmers and farming in which case you should (a) sue for divorce so as to get half of the farm assets before their value sinks even lower, or (b) get psychiatric help to cure you of associating with bums and losers.

If you scored less than three, you should read the rest of this book so as to more completely understand how lucky you are that (a) you didn't buy a farm, (b) you didn't inherit a farm, and/or (c) you didn't marry a farmer.

Figure 3: DEFICIENCY PAYMENT
As detailed in chapter twenty-one, "The Theory and Practice of Farming."

◀ twenty-two ▶

Weather Goest Thou?

While farmers eventually learn to laugh at machine break-downs and the million-and-one things that go wrong, weather has always stopped them cold.

There isn't a machine made that can't be fixed eventually. But when crops need moisture and it doesn't rain, there's no fixing the problem. If it hails on that mythical perfect crop, there's no fixing the problem. And if it rains during harvest instead of shining bright, there's no fixing that one either.

As a consequence, farmers spend a lot of time worrying and talking about the weather. Farmers are experts at talking about weather.

This preoccupation with weather has until now been a blight on the social life of farmers. It used to be that anyone who talked weather was thought to have a brain like a weather balloon, filled with helium. As a consequence, farmers were easily spotted at all social gatherings by their harping on about the weather. It didn't take long for people to assume that because farmers talked about the weather, they were morons.

All this has now changed. The reason for the change is that weather is the hot new social topic. Everybody's talking weather.

Why weather is winning on the talk charts is because it's so unpredictable. Scientists are concerned that the weather is getting more erratic. We now get summer in winter, and winter in spring. We get tornadoes where we shouldn't, and no snow where we should. People are interested. In some sense they're talking about weather as if their lives depended on it—just like farmers.

Now that this weather stuff is trendy in good homes, anyone who can talk weather is allowed into the better salons around the country.

The problem is that while the sophisticated can quickly distinguish between heliumheads and weather-whizzes (and as a consequence, avoid witherheads), the farmer can't. Farmers don't have the experience to do so. Historically, talking about the weather has always been farmers' entrée into conversation. And as I've pointed out, until recently it has also been the reason for farmers being excluded from most manner of socializing. Their absence from the social scene has meant that stubble jumpers haven't learned how to separate dunderheads from thunderheads. The result is that the average farmer jumps right into a conversation when he hears "weather," only to find himself, more often than not, listening to some ninny talk about nothing when the farmer had been hoping to have someone talk about El Nino.

How can a farmer separate the wheat from the chaff, so to speak? Well my own solution, far from perfect mind you, is a whether quiz. Whether I talk to people depends on whether they pass. Here are the questions I ask. Try it and see whether your weather comprehension is good enough to make intelligent small talk with a farmer.

1. ENSO
   (a) is the Fonz' half-brother
   (b) stands for El Nino-Southern Oscillation
   (c) stands for Eh Numbscull Snowin' Out

If you guessed (a), score zero. If you guessed (b), score one. If you guessed (c), score two. (Since our weather is all screwed up, simple observation is better than complex theory.)

2. An Isobar
   (a) serves cold liquor
   (b) has something to do with pressure

If you guessed (a), score two. If you guessed (b), score one. If you know where the Iso Bar is located, order two.

3. A surface depression
   (a) has something to do with the weather
   (b) describes a bad day for you
   (c) is what your body makes on the ground after coming out of the Iso Bar

If you guessed (a), score one. If you guessed (b), score zero. If you landed on (c), subtract two.

4. A castellatus is
   (a) a line of altocumulus clouds
   (b) a band leader who plays nice music

Score one and one. He plays at the Iso Bar.

5. Diurnal variation refers to
   (a) the relative heights of the plumbing in the men's washroom at the Iso Bar
   (b) air temperature

If you guessed (a), subtract two. (You're beginning to spend so much time in that place I doubt you'd know anything about the weather.) If you guessed air temperature, score one.

If you scored between two and four, you are a witherhead. Farmers will ignore you everywhere. Memorize the next chapter.

If you scored five or six, you're probably one of the guys. And as one of the new weatherheads, farmers will always talk to you. Skip the next chapter.

If you scored seven, you're probably a fellow farmer. In that case, right after we talked about the weather and wheat prices, the first thing I'd ask you is, "Are you interested in buying another farm?"

twenty-three

Weather Thou Goest
—I Follow

Don't know as much about the weather as a farmer does, eh? I'm not surprised. Although most nonfarmers spend nearly as much time griping about the weather as a farmer does, nonfarmers are amazingly uninformed about the stuff.

There's a reason for this. Knowledge is based on information. Most people base their weather knowledge on the prognostications of weather forecasters in the belief that meteorologists, being experts, know what they're doing. Wrong-o.

Farmers know better. Farmers have learned some painful lessons about experts over the years.[1] They've learned that today's expert advice is tomorrow's folly. When it comes to weather, farmers have learned that a forecast predicting a

---

1. The lessons learned from weather forecasters have all been minor-league inconveniences compared with the lessons learned at the hands of agricultural experts.

90 percent chance of rain is a guarantee of continued drought. Nonfarmers don't often notice the difference between the prediction of rain and the pouring of rain. People whose lives don't depend on the weather seldom pay much attention to it. As a consequence, they don't keep track of the batting average of weather forecasters.

Statistics show that Canada's meteorologists are accurate 80 percent of the time. At first glance this seems like a pretty good average. The fact is, however, that at least 80 percent of Canadians seem to live in that 20 percent error zone. The inescapable conclusion is that the majority of Canadians are basing their weather knowledge on weather forecasting which is nearly always wrong. That being the case it's no wonder Canadian weather smarts are at an all-time low. Canadian weather knowledge is based on the rantings of Ouija board specialists trying to predict rain.

I think the problem with professional forecasting lies with a misunderstanding of weather basics, to wit: forecasters don't seem to understand weather proverbs. It goes without saying that if meteorologists don't understand basic truths about weather which have been honed and handed down for generations, their forecasting of the weather won't be particularly accurate. I once read a magazine article written by a meteorologist explaining why certain proverbs were right or wrong. And while he was 80 percent correct as to whether the proverbs were right, his interpretations of the maxims were all wrong.[1]

The consequence of such proverbial ignorance from the experts is weather illiteracy in the general population. As with language illiteracy, people are missing the basics. Without the basics it's impossible to take in those weather refinements that will make your small talk the hot new front in any social conversation.

So how are you going to upgrade from witherhead to

---

1. This 80 percent business only goes to prove that when meteorologists are wrong, they're consistently 80 percent wrong.

weatherhead? How can you be at the cutting edge of shop talk at your next dinner party? How can you match wits with a farmer's weather witticisms?

You've got to learn to fake it. And to help you do that, I've listed some of the more-common weather proverbs and their applications as seen from a farmer's point of view as well as his yard. I suggest you memorize these babies so as to appear knowledgeable about weather at your next encounter with a farmer.

1. If the groundhog sees his shadow on February 2, there'll be six more weeks of winter; if he doesn't see his shadow, spring is near. *True or false?*

   False. Groundhogs aren't stupid enough to show themselves on February 2 in the prairies because they know there'll be at least six more weeks of winter in Canada and up to three more months of winter in the prairies.

2. The last twelve days of January rule the weather for the whole year. *True or false?*

   This one is simply a typo. The question should be a statement and the statement should read, "The last twelve days of January are enough to ruin your whole year."

3. A red sky at night is a sailor's delight; a red sky at morning is a sailor's warning. *True or false?*

   True if you're a sailor. False if you're a farmer. Any sky is a warning of disaster to a farmer. (See Magoo and Murphy.)

4. Squirrels gather more nuts before a severe winter. *True or false?*

   False. This statement is just another typo. The question was originally a statement and read, "Anyone who isn't nutty after a severe winter is at least a little squirrelly."

5. During prairie winters, it can get too cold to snow. *True or false?*

   True. During prairie winters it can get too cold to do anything.

6. The first frost comes with a full moon. *True or false?*

   False. The first frost comes somewhere in the middle of July which is, strangely enough, the approximate date of the last frost of the previous winter.

7. When there's dew upon the grass, rain will never come to pass. *True or false?*

   True. Except you don't need the first part of the rhyme. All you ever have to remember about farming, is that if rain is needed, it will never come to pass.

   Once you've committed these gems to memory you're well on your way to mingling with the prairie stubble set. May I make one more suggestion that will add to your believability? Begin wearing a baseball cap with the name of some obscure farm chemical emblazoned on it, and go around muttering "This is nothing compared to '56," next time you step out for the evening.

twenty-four

Where Farmers
Are Appreciated

While farmer types are just beginning to be appreciated in the city because of their weather smarts, we've been appreciated near to death in small towns for other reasons. Just how great that appreciation is came home to me last year during our local version of Farmer Appreciation Week.[1]

It all began when the mayor called up. He and the towns-people had decided that being as it was Farmer Apprecia-tion Week, they should do something to show their solidarity with the local farmers. He informed me that a gala event was planned for the next day.

Well seeing is believing, so I headed for town to catch the action. It turned out that the town had hired a few bodies under some federal hire-a-body programme to cut grass, trim hedges, and in general beautify the town prior to the big

---

1. Farmer Appreciation Week is the payment of lip service to farmers in place of payment of service to farmers.

event. I hadn't even got out of the car when someone came over and asked me for a donation to help stage the affair and cover the town's cost of hiring the government-subsidized labour.

My wallet had barely cooled down when somebody else came by and announced that all the hired bodies had quit because the work was too demeaning.

The mayor was quick on his toes. He called for a meeting to be held in the town hall. There he noted that it would be a shame not to go ahead with plans to appreciate the local farmers. He pointed out that since most of the farmers to be appreciated were present,[1] it was only fair if we all pitched in to help beautify the town for the celebration.

It was voted on and found to be fair. (I noticed all my fellow farmers abstained.) So we farmers all went home for different tools and came back to clean up the town. I ended up fixing a leaky eaves trough on the mayor's house, and a couple of my neighbours cut a few hedges and then levelled a few gardens with their front-end loaders. We all cut lots and lots of lawns.

Later that evening after we had finished all the work, the mayor took up a collection from us for supper, and then sent someone out with my pickup to buy some pizzas.

After the pizza the mayor announced we still had to plan the activities for our local Farmer Appreciation Day (although to tell the truth, I would have appreciated going home to bed rather than staying up to figure out some way to appreciate myself).

During all the scheduling, the mayor pointed out that since it doesn't cost anything for farmers to grow their own food, and since the town was in rough shape financially, it would only be fair if all the farmers brought food for the celebration. And he asked if we farmers, being such inventors, would mind working up a few skits and songs for a little

---

1. Like me, they too believed that seeing is believing when it comes to people doing something free for farmers.

entertainment afterwards. Then he went home.

It was pretty late by the time we farmers worked out our little show, so we were all pretty tired when we got up at 5:00 the next morning to get the pancake breakfast ready. I was so tired I forgot to pay my $2 for breakfast until the mayor reminded me.

The only people who looked bright-eyed and bushy-tailed were the politicians who were running around appreciating everybody. It may be ungrateful of me to mention this, but it appeared to me that the mayor, a couple of local MLAs, and our MP appreciated the donations they were soliciting even more than they were appreciating the farmers from whom they were soliciting donations.

The whole thing was in the paper the next morning, right beside a picture of the mayor, the MP, and both MLAs. The MP said his little extravaganza was a total success. The mayor went on to say how the townspeople had enjoyed doing something for the farmers for a change, and how the pioneer spirit still wasn't dead. And the MLAs pointed out how it is still possible to be nice and make a profit. It turned out that with the $2 charge for the breakfast we farmers cooked, the $5 for the supper we provided, and the $3 for the variety show we performed, the town made a $350 profit.

What was it that one of those old time soldier-philosopher-kings said about it being better to be feared than loved? . . .

◀ twenty-five ▶

The Price of Appreciation

Being appreciated does different things to different people. Some are moved by accolades; some are bashful when singled out for praise; farmers become sceptical when anyone wants to do something for them. History justifies this scepticism.

Real farmers are particularly sceptical of anything done to or for anyone living west of Ontario by anyone living east of Manitoba.

I used to think that western distrust of anything devised or built east of Manitoba was just a knee-jerk reaction to the benign actions of Ottawa, a Skinnerian response to some unintended slight which happened to land on a farmer.[1] Imagine my surprise when I uncovered fact to this fiction.

The uncovering began at my doctor's office. I'd stopped in because of a rash on my right leg. Doctor John only glanced at my leg. It was my pants he examined carefully.

---

1. Something like automatically beginning to cuss at a machine the instant it breaks down even before knowing what's wrong with it.

I remember him sticking a finger through a hole in my right pocket before shaking his head and muttering, "looney rash."

At first I thought he had *loony virus*, but it turns out that in fact our looney is what caused my rash. He assured me I wasn't the first patient he and other prairie doctors had examined this past winter with this problem.

He said a sudden rash of unexplained rashes had caused doctors profound puzzlement. Specialists were called in. Nothing was discovered. The unravelling began as a result of the rantings of a few farmers who swore up and down that the new loonies were to blame. Well, the physicians were at their wits' end, so in desperation they subjected the loonies to chemical analysis. Again they found nothing. It was a physics professor who discovered what the problem was. He studied the phenomenon and made his report: it was the large size and consequent heat-holding capabilities of the looney which were to blame for the rash. He demonstrated that the looney could cause first-degree burns and scarring on naked flesh if the coin was either colder than $-40°$ C or hotter than $40°$ C. He'd measured the burn-level point in looney TUNES (Temperature Units Needed for Exposure to Scald).

Once this effect was documented, doctors began agitating Canadian weather offices to include a looney TUNES warning when those critical temperatures were expected.

That's when the sinister intent of the looney became apparent and justified every evil thought every farmer had ever had about anyone living east of Manitoba.

It all began when a janitor at the weather office pointed out that the only place the temperature ever exceeded plus or minus $40°$ C was the prairies.

Farmers were quick to note they were the only class of citizens who were traditionally known to have holes in their work clothes, and who would work even when it was hotter or colder than plus or minus $40°$ C.

The deduction was obvious. The looney was designed to

harass farmers and mark the west as separate from the rest of Canada.

Two University of Saskatchewan graduate students looking for a quick and easy research paper brought more of the sinister plot to the fore. Their research indicated that whenever one of these super-heated or -cooled coins touched a person, that person let out a howl much like a loon. In a second double-blind study, the psychologists discovered that their test subjects judged anyone making such a howl to be loony (something all farmers have long thought all Easterners have thought about all farmers). The implications were enormous—farmers were being needlessly harassed by the federal government.

All would have died down if three secret memos hadn't been leaked to the press. Once they came to light, the situation became public knowledge and made relations between the federal government and farmers even more tense than before. The memos provided an insight into government meddling hitherto unheard of in Canada.

The memos documented a plan whereby the looney was introduced with the hope that looney burns would cause physicians and Canadians to think farmers were suffering from psychosomatic rashes. Once the Canadian Medical Association and the Canadian public were convinced that farmers were unhinged, the plan called for the government to attempt one of two final solutions to the farm problem.

The first part of the plan (the so-called "Final Solution"), was to have farmers committed to institutions by doctors willing to sign committal papers for farmers. A detailed cost-run analysis showed it was cheaper to incarcerate a farmer in a mental institution than to subsidize his farming habit.

The second part of the plan was dubbed the "Final Final Solution." It began where the Final Solution ended. The "Final Final Solution" was simply to ignore whichever farmers weren't locked up in the first dragnet. The raison d'être was that in the event of continuing droughts and/or low grain prices, the government expected public support

81

when it called the still-farming farmers crazy and told them to get lost.

A call from western farm groups to the prime minister's office demanding an explanation of the memos has resulted only in a terse message calling everything a coincidence.

The cause of western alienation advanced one hundred years.

◀ twenty-six ▶

Latin Mottoes

So why do farmers think Easterners kick sand in our faces? *Do* Easterners kick sand in the faces of farmers? That's as close to philosophy as real farmers get out here on the back 40. I think our feelings of insecurity come about because Easterners are secure about their place in the sun, and we farmers aren't. It's not just that they feel superior to us humble stubble jumpers, it's also that we feel inferior.

Americans have long known about superiority. They inherently believe in their superiority. Phrases define the American psyche and hold it in place against the rest of the world. "Better dead than red." "America: love it or leave it." "Mother, God, and apple pie." Catchy phrases like that are a vaccination against inferiority.

Maybe not so strangely, we farmers here in the west lack catchy phrases.[1] It's true. Unlike the rest of Canada, the Prairie provinces don't have official mottoes. We don't have any great words to live by. We don't even have mediocre words to exist by.

---

1. Could this be another federal plot to harass the west?

People like catchy phrases. They tend to identify with them. In the absence of mottoes, we western farmers have nothing to identify with so we get defensive and feel positively inferior compared to our Latinized neighbours.

Consider that Ontario has the motto, *Ut Incepit Fidelis Sic Permanet* ("Loyal she began, loyal she remains"). Notice how this Latin limerick fits the upper Canadian miasma. They always have been the big cheese. They've always been loyal to themselves. And who can accuse Ontarians of feeling inferior?

Only Alberta, Saskatchewan, and Manitoba don't have official mottoes. And look at the negative light in which the rest of the country views us farmers. All we're perceived to identify with are grain, cattle, and Wayne Gretzky. Cattle and grain prices are always unstable, and Gretzky was shipped south of the border.

No wonder we stubble jumpers are seen as being inferior and acting defensively. And more's the pity, we don't even have a Latin one-liner to come back with against our accusers.

The only way out, as I see it, is the adoption of some Latin limericks for Saskatchewan and company. Something regal, befitting our new status as followers of the good life in Canada.

Historically, the only motto that western farmers ever had was, "Please sir, can I have more?"

Given the increasing militancy of Alberta, that simple supplication should now be reinterpreted and translated into Albertanese as, "MORE SIR. MORE." While it must be granted that this is in keeping with Albertan philosophy, it ain't Latin and it ain't regal. Consider how genteel this maxim becomes when translated into Latin, *Grabius maximus; negotiaba remainderia* ("Grab everything you can; negotiate for the rest"). The Latin is just so much more refined.

In Saskatchewan we still retain a strong rural flavour and while we haven't become quite so aggressive as Alberta, we have increased our complaining to very audible levels. I

suggest something catchy like, *Nastius tempus vos* _____
which roughly translated means, "Tough times what with
_____." The blank left at the motto's end enables
current issues such as interest rates, drought, hoppers, or
government to be inserted as needed.

And since Manitoba marks the eastern terminus of the
west, what else could the Manitoba motto be but *Westus
maximus; eastus minimus* ("The West is best; the East is a
beast.").

Hurling these churlish Latin raspberries at the Laputian
shadow of upper Canadian economic and cultural conquest
hovering over us will help in straightening the bent back-
bone of western farmers to new heights of disrespect.

twenty-seven

Roots by Any Other Name Are Still Hard to Pick Up

There's more to self-assuredness than mere words of course. Even though farmers' self-images will improve immeasurably after adopting fitting words of wisdom to live by, we'll need more than phrases before we take our rightful place in the sun. We'll need confirmation that our roots and lineage are of noble extraction. If we can put together a heady combination of fine phrases and forefathers, we too can become as sanctimonious and insufferable as the nouveau riche or the recently titled. In short we'll be just like Easterners. And then, like everyone else with money and position (meaning Easterners), we'll take up federal politics.

First of course, we have to research our regal roots; find our fabled foreflushers.

I've been looking into this ancestral roots business. What I found there shocked even me. Believe it or not, farmers and farming trace themselves back to the best of ancient

Greece and Rome. The roots of Western civilization just don't go back a heck of a lot further than that. (And people talk about tracing their roots back to the Mayflower as being noteworthy!)

We farmers can unblushingly state: we are the forefathers of all Olympic athletes (who were, after all, the best of our forefathers, and whose culture has so shaped western thought).

It's no coincidence that the Olympics and harvest both occur in late summer. And the reason it's no coincidence is because the Olympics are a direct descendant of farming methods. Scouts' honour. It's the truth.

Everyone knows that the ancient decathlon is the fore-runner of all individual Olympic events. What everyone doesn't know is that the decathlon is a descendant of ancient agrarian practices which were collectively known as the "farmathlon."

It has to be a given maxim that you must eat before you can exercise. Therefore it's safe to say that farming must predate the Olympics. As for the proof that the Olympics are a descendant of farming practices, consider . . .

Even the Olympic cry of farther, further, and faster has its origins in farming—farther in debt, further commodity declines, and faster-rising costs.

Indeed it's quite easy to prove that modern farming practices still have in them the origins of every event in the modern Olympics.

Consider the hurdles, and the speed with which a farmer can hop across swathes in an effort to stop a combine which is rolling backwards, downhill, and out of control.

And if you've ever repaired a machine only to have it recommit suicide ten seconds after starting up, you'll understand where the hammer throw comes from.

Similarly the javelin was invented by a farmer who found an old fence post jammed into the threshing cylinder of his combine. Being a reasonable man, he threw the damn thing as far away as he could.

The steeple chase is a direct offshoot of some farmer charging across a machine-strewn yard after noticing a grain auger was continuing to fill an already full bin.

Ever wonder why relays involve handoffs and are run in heats? Watch farmers under the broiling heat of an August sun as they relay tools, parts, and information back and forth, in and out of a broken-down combine.

Jumping events. Ever try to chase a mad cow from a lush crop back into a parched pasture only to have the cow chase you over the nearest fence? That sport is known today as high jump. (It takes no intuitive leap of logic to visualize inventing the pole vault for really high fences.)

The whole body of gymnastics came about when some farmer inadvertently stepped backwards off a grain truck. Subsequent and kinder generations added water to the sport, and thus began tower diving.

And how about the scenario of a farmer racing a raincloud back to her open granaries. In driving the most direct route (which just happens to run through a slough bottom), she gets stuck. Her continuing run on foot and in the rain sprinkled with the forced jumping of puddles is well known in the modern Olympics as cross-country running.

I could go on, but I'm sure you get the picture. Farmers are thee ancient Olympians. Such noble ancestry is the perfect spoon with which to swallow our inferiority for all time.

Once we become masters of our own destinies, then like all self-appointed philosopher-kings, we shall be able to fulfil those destinies—meaning we farmers will go into politics and do unto others what others have been doing unto us.

◀ twenty-eight ▶

Farmophones

Farmers are the original philosopher-kings. All have their own land, their own castle, and their own point of view. All enjoy telling each other, or anybody else they can corner for that matter, how to run their lives. While farmers like philosophy, they love politics. It's true. They will talk about politics nearly as much as about the weather, or about farming, hockey, or hunting, which is to say, quite a lot.

We farmers can now point backwards in antiquity to our noble roots and upwards with our middle finger and fine phrases to Easterners. That being the case, farmers in all provinces will soon rally to the cry of "It's election time, folks." Since I'm a Saskabusher and know the Saskatchewan psyche better than that of other provinces, it's the Saskabusher farmer, philosopher, and future parliamentarian whose future I'll speculate about.

The Saskatchewan of yesterday is the ancestral home of the CCF and such entrenched social programmes as medicare. Farmers were leaders in both these movements. There was no francophone or anglophone lobbying or leading here, just the application of common sense.

More and more these days, politics seems to be a struggle for anglophone or francophone superiority. Quite frankly, I'm tired of all this *phone* business. And what good have the present-day anglophones and francophones done for Canada?

Remember Pierre the franco-anglophone? He gave us a constitution that has given Canadian unity a bad case of constipation; a constitution which is about as stirring as a puffed wheat cake recipe. Remember Meech Lake? Meech was an effort by Brian, the anglo-francophone, to coordinate all political parties of parliament and all provincial premiers in uniting the country. Instead of uniting the country, that all-party attempt at harmony drove the wedge in deeper.

In short, the political players, those all-party anglophone and francophone wunderkids, blew it.

The time is ripe to take the *phones* away from the kids. In particular, restricting party leaders to an anglophone-francophone choice is like restricting a farmer to a choice between two different pickups.

There are many pickups. Correspondingly, there are many *phones*. What about all those unemployophones, unionophones, and small businessophones out there to name only a few? They also speak the language of Canada.

I say that whether a party leader's first language is anglo or franco is far less meaningful than whether he or she is willing to talk things out. After all, language is only important if it's used to communicate. And what farmer isn't always ready to communicate? What we need is a PM who'll talk to us, not at us. We need a farmophone.

Yup. It's time for a change; time for a return to political grassroots. (Who knows more about grassroots than a farmer?) It's time all party leaders were elected from a slate of farmophones.

Farmers even have many of the desirable attributes politicians need.

Politicians think they are big wheels because they govern

big tracts of land. Farmers have always driven big wheels around in big circles. Farmers are accustomed to big tracts of land. A farmophone would be a natural for the PM's job and the travel it entails because farmers are used to travelling around a lot to look for enough extra jobs to support their farming habit.

Politicians have to talk to a lot of people and string a lot of bull. If you've ever been at coffee row, you'd know a farmer has that ability down pat.

And in the event a farmer doesn't get elected, "no problem." Farmers are always known for their *maybe-next-year* attitude. Political survival demands resiliency.

Any farmer with a bent for politics would take Canada by storm on a farmophone ticket. Most of us are used to deficit financing. This puts us on a par with the best Bay Street bankers. Our poverty puts us on the same level as pooro-phones, unemployophones, and direstraightophones. And since these *phones* make up the majority of the Canadian voting public, this should give any farmophone ticket the common manophone vote to put him or her in bed at 24 Sussex Drive.

Figure 4: SCREWDRIVER
As detailed in chapter twenty-one, "The Theory and Practice of Farming."

◀ twenty-nine ▶

The Price of
Political Involvement

There is, of course, a price to pay to put farm power in the driver's seat of parliament—involvement. Putting up posters. Knocking on doors. Mailing flyers.

You don't get your boy or girl in if you don't hustle on the hustings. To elect a king or queen, you've got to sell that king or queen, give them lots of exposure to the Canadian public.

Believe it or not, I've found it possible to have too much exposure to politics. So much so, that I absolutely shy away from the democratic process these days.

I've always thought of political posters like warts, something every sensible human can quite nicely live without. The first-time election of Brian's boys to power brought the devil to my doorstep in a big way. It all began the day the election was called those many years ago. All the party candidates had come courting that first day. All of them wanted me to join their party. At first I'd been flattered. It was only when my lawns got flattened that I realized the grim truth. They didn't want to convert me. They only wanted to plant political posters in my petunias because my lawn and flower bed are within reading distance of the highway. It became almost like the crusades what with local politicians taking up their colours and throwing down the opposition's. I vowed never again.

Time heals all wounds.

Time is also the mother of revenge. After four years of scheming I figured out what I thought was a sure-fire method of preventing political pests from pounding posts and pinning pictures in my petunias of people posing for parliament. I was ready when the next election was called. I put on a dress, high heels, and black mesh tights and waited for the political hordes to descend. I reasoned that if I demonstrated a concern only for the latest colours in women's clothing, maybe the local politicians would forget trying to fit blue, red, and orange colours on my lawn again.

I was feeling just a trifle self-conscious in my new dress so I decided to read the newspaper to divert my self-awareness while I waited for the politicians to appear. That's when I noticed an article from south of the border describing a new technique in fighting the alarming increase in sexual offences. The convicted offenders are made to put a sign on their lawn indicating to the world that they are convicted sex offenders.

Being a bit of a philosopher, I immediately began pondering the parallel between feeling pressured to put up election signs and the forced declarations of deviancy.

I hadn't got far in my deliberations when I heard a knock at the door. It was all three of the local politicians. They took one look at me before deciding they were double-parked in an ambulance zone.

To make a long story short, I was arrested and charged with sexual deviancy. I tried to explain to the judge that I had only put on the dress so as to avoid the all-party pressures to plant political posters. It was a bad suggestion. The judge must have read the same newspaper I had. He sentenced me to put a sign on my lawn saying I was a sexual deviant.

Where political posters had earlier been my enemy, they suddenly became my saviour. To avoid election signs on my lawn I had turned to deviancy. Now to avoid deviancy signs on my lawn I would have to resort to political billboards. I quickly pounded a number of all-party posters around that deviancy sign.

The whole affair left me with one determination. I want no more exposure to politics.

thirty

Wheat Wars Are Nasti Things

And if past elections haven't been enough to deconvert me from a political career, a magazine story I've just happened on has absolutely convinced me that I want nothing more to do with politics any time, any way, or any place.

According to this magazine article, we farmers were inadvertent players in a political strategy that almost changed the course of the world.

The story began a number of years ago when the Pentagon put together a think-tank named New Age Science, Technology, and Invention (NASTI) to develop exotic war toys. There were some strange war strategies invented as a consequence of those NASTIs folding the leading edges of their different disciplines together. They combined the latest research developments into the real, the unreal, and the visionary, and shoved the result into a computer bigger than a rock star's ego.

The most bizarre project they hit upon was the invention of a nondetectable way of killing grain crops — aimed at the commies of course. We all know people whose green thumb

96

is the kiss of death to plants. These NASTIs devised a war strategy utilizing that human plant-killing essence. The NASTIs first isolated the *Attila the Hun* plant-killing ability which exists in certain people. With that knowledge, the NASTIs then focused their efforts toward turning others into plant killers. And they wanted to do this in a way the Soviets wouldn't be able to detect. They wanted to win the cold war before the Soviets even knew war had been waged.

Their development procedure was right out of science fiction.

Their whole discovery hinged on crystals. On this the NASTIs were far ahead of their time. It's only been in the last few years that New Age theorists in California have discovered crystal power.

The NASTIs discovered that among humans, the most potent plant killers were crystal shaped, fat in the middle, and pointed at both ends. Once this discovery was made, the rest was easy.

The process they used to turn people into weapons to wipe out wheat makes fascinating history. No one will be surprised when I say these NASTIs used the whole of North America as their testing ground. How they did so is quite intriguing.

First they had to find a way to build the optimum crystal shape into the general population.

They invented junk food.

Next they had to discover a way of getting the general population to ingest the plant-killing gene which they had isolated.

They blended the solution with beer.

Time passed. These human weapons were built up to optimal shape and ability—ready to be unleashed.

And finally the NASTIs had to discover a way to get their plant killers onto Soviet soil.

The NASTIs eased cold-war tensions by offering to foot the bill for green stamps for all airline tickets to the U.S.S.R. The Russian bear accepted this Trojan horse offering at face value and responded by opening its arms to the Western world.

The NASTIs began an ad campaign to sell the merits of travel in the U.S.S.R. And just as hordes of fat crystal-shaped tourists were signing up to see the wonders of life behind the Iron Curtain, the unexpected happened. The Berlin wall came tumbling down and in doing so, prevented what might have become the strangest nondeclared war in history. The Wheat War was put on hold because the NASTIs believed the collapse of the Berlin wall spelled *auf Wiedersehen* for classical Communism. Their argument for inaction was a good one. By avoiding anything to do with destabilizing the Soviet bloc, the Americans would avoid becoming a focus for any possible movement to rebuild Soviet Communism. The Pentagon was convinced that Soviet destabilization will happen on its own, and when it does, the Yanks will be there for the garage sale.

This whole clandestine operation proves that farmers can be pawns in big-time political circles—whether we want to be or not. There's no doubting that history would've blamed the farmers had this war game been played to its conclusion.

If I wasn't sure before, I am now—politics is as hard to get away from as farming. I can only wonder if politicians have their own verse to the farmer's lament, "My grain is a headache."

thirty-one

Winterization

What with work, play, politics, and being a bit player in the odd world conspiracy, farming goes on at a hectic pace. Even the onset of that dreaded nemesis, winter, doesn't spell slow-down on the back 40.

Take for instance the annual rite of winterization, whereby everything that has been used all summer must be taken apart, stored, or hidden until the next year.

Putting my sailboat away for the year is a perfect example of the difference between urban and rural winterization.

A city slicker simply slides his sailboat sedately sideways from sidewalk to shop some Saturday. If only I had it so easy.

The complication of rural winterization arises because everything on a farm has to do double duty. Sailboats are no exception. I built my boat out of odd pieces either I or my neighbours didn't need at the time, knowing full well that when the time came, the odd pieces would have to go back to their original duties.

When you consider the effort I expend in putting my sailboat away, you'll understand why I dread the winterization process nearly as much as I dread winter itself.

A good anchor on a sailboat is a must. (Being able to keep a sailboat in one place is just as important as making it go someplace else.) My best anchor, which started life as a cultivator shovel, has to be rebolted to my cultivator for fall work.

The sails are no big problem. They simply go back into my house and on the bed where they belong. The boat cushions go back on the chesterfield. And all the ropes go back to become the clothesline again.

The mast is a little more complicated. I borrow it from a neighbour. The mast is nothing but a big pipe. However, it has to be hooked up to the water pump so that her cattle can have water through the winter. In exchange for borrowing the mast all summer, I lend her my boat all winter. So the boat itself has to be thoroughly cleaned out because it doubles as the winter cattle trough. (After all, if a boat can keep water out all summer, it should be able to keep water in all winter.)

I loan the boat trailer out as a sleigh during the winter for hauling bales, so the wheels have to come off. And since they're ground grips, they go on an old tractor I borrow to push snow. I get the tractor in exchange for loaning the boat trailer. Speaking of snow, I put the rudder in the porch for that terrible moment when I have to shovel my sidewalk.

And the oars go into the chicken coop so the chickens can have something to roost on during the long winter nights.

I'm not sure I'll go with an outboard auxiliary next year. Seems harvest always starts before sailing finishes. It takes almost a whole day to disassemble my put-together outboard and put the motor back on my grain auger where it belongs. Fortunately, it doesn't take very long to move the night running lights from my sailboat to the back of my grain truck.

This year I've got one additional task left before I welcome the first snowfall. Somehow I've got to get all the paint off the boat and onto my barn where it was supposed to go. Any suggestions?

thirty-two

Getting There Is Half the Fun When You Discover It's Twice the Cost

Is there life after winterization? If not, at least there's winter. Winter is the time of year farmers live for; the time of year when all farmers go away on holidays to fish or play in the water—unless they have to feed cattle, haul grain, fix machinery, or take a winter job so as to pay some of the bills so as to continue farming.

Last year I overcame all the minor obstacles of work and money and finally discovered the secret of getting away on holidays in the winter so as to fish or play in the water.

Overcoming the work obstacle was easy. I simply ignored all the work I had to do.

Finding enough money for this mythical winter vacation was a little more complicated.

101

I thought I'd solved the money angle last year when I learned how to forgo the cost of personal winterization — new clothes and boots, and enough antifreeze to make me forget about winter — and apply the savings toward a winter holiday.

A warm-weather holiday is something I've been scheming about for years, but due to chronic personal insolvency, I've never been able to afford a winter holiday in a warm climate.

I was able to take that holiday last year after discovering, in the course of a single summer evening, how to apply the intricacies of deficit financing as practised by the federal government to my own humble station in life.[1] The understanding caused a sudden blinding flash of economic enlightenment — I could afford a holiday.

The big problem I traditionally had to face in wanting to go someplace exotic was airfare. Airfare always seemed to run a trifle more than the price of the few gallons of gas I pour into Spot's gas tank every week. I knew that getting to the tropics was going to cost big bucks, anywhere up to two thousand of them.

Last year I had a monthly budget of $1,000 that couldn't be tampered with. I knew I couldn't afford to spend $2,000 for a month in paradise. Indeed I knew I couldn't afford to spend $2,000 last year in any month for anything. However, with the aid of my newly acquired economic insight, I could see that if I were to stay two months in paradise, then I would be spending only $1,000 a month on travel. All of this pointed toward the possibility of an even longer holiday than I thought I could afford, assuming I could figure out some way to eat and put an occasional hotel roof over my head.

Next I took the $600 I would foolishly have spent on winter clothes and boots (and enough antifreeze to make me forget about winter), and applied the money against the two months proposed for paradise. My travel budget was thus

---

1. An economist friend of mine and a dozen beer were instrumental in explaining the footwork to me.

reduced to just $700 a month (after all you don't need over-shoes in paradise).

Some late-night study revealed that it was realistic to budget an Asian holiday for $15 a day, or $450 a month. And since I budget $25 a day ($750 a month) on the farm for food and incidentals, I was actually saving $300 a month by travelling. This brought my travel budget down to an estimated $400 a month.

January and February are our coldest months, and the months I decided to travel. With an empty house, I saved money on heating. With my thermostat set at a constant 10° C, I saved $50 a month in heating costs—which reduced the cost of my trip to only $350 a month.

And of course my absence reduced my phone and electricity bills too. The savings amounted to nearly $100 a month. And because I saw a couple of farms during my trip, I was able to write part of the trip off as a business expense on my income tax.

In short, it turned out that I couldn't afford not to take that holiday. If I stayed home I'd have spent a fortune in comparison. So holidaying I went. Quite frankly, I enjoyed fishing and playing in the water a lot. I had a wonderful time. I'd intended to make it a yearly affair.

Alas, my return to the old homestead wasn't quite so wonderful. In spite of the fact that on paper, at least, I had saved a fortune, the cupboard was bare when I returned home.

So much for my brief fling with deficit financing.

So much for my brief fling with exotic vacations in the winter.

Perchance there are some deficiencies in this deficit-financing business which I haven't figured out yet.

◀ thirty-three ▶

Real Farmers Glide Through Winter

Even though I occasionally look at my slides from that wonderful trip, I've found it best not to look at my atlas too often. Although misery may like company, I can assure you misery would rather take another exotic vacation.

There is a bright side to all this I suppose. Even though I may not be able to afford travelling, I still have winters off, which is better than not being able to afford travelling and not having winters off.

Which means I've learned to do what I always do, stay home in the winter to curl or play hockey. The truth is, though, most of my farmer friends and I have about given up on curling. Old-timer hockey has really caught on in its place. What with the rush to stay in shape, more and more farmers are tying on their hockey skates and using their curling brooms to clean the grain boxes on their grain trucks.

No doubt about it, Old-timer hockey is the sport of the

decade. There are now more farmers playing Old-timer hockey than cheating on their income tax. Some farmers take their hockey so seriously they won't even drink before the game; so seriously that in some farm leagues, they even keep track of wins, losses, and goals, and hand out trophies after games instead of beer.

Even though Old-timer hockey is the rage, its attractions are about as arcane as the attractions of farming. Since this is a book about farmers and what they do, it's only fitting I explain everything they do. The following is an explanation of Old-timer hockey and its significance to farmers.

The Game   Old-timer farm hockey is to real farm hockey what pillow-fighting is to war. The pace of Old-timer farm hockey is comparable to real farm hockey played in knee-deep water.

The Players   A hockey farmer becomes an Old-timer when *post hoc, ergo propter hoc* ("after hockey he goes from proper hockey") and when he has more years behind him than hairs on top of him. A farm hockey team becomes an Old-timer's farm team when the combined weight of any six of them is great enough that they must weigh in at all highway scales.

History   Old-timer hockey came about as the result of an amendment to Bill C–22 (Abolition of Hockey Bill). Historical records from that period show Bill C–22 was introduced by Revenue Canada via the prime minister's office.

Revenue Canada began the push to abolish hockey when a farm wife and hockey widow tearfully called up and pointed out that with the demise of her husband during a hockey game, she couldn't pay their taxes. The thought of death being one more tax loophole that rich farmers could hide behind sent the whole of Revenue Canada into a tizzy and resulted in a call to abolish hockey. A bizarre sidelight to this hysterical moment was actually responsible for the "Old-timer" amendment to the "Hockey Abolition" Bill C–22. Apparently the woman misread the telephone number through her tears and called the French service of Revenue

Canada by mistake. Montreal was winning in the Stanley Cup series that year. As a compromise to Revenu Canada Impot and the French, the government decided not to abolish, but simply to emasculate hockey for older and wealthier farmers and thereby prevent the further use of hockey death as farm-tax avoidance. Such emasculation resulted in the "Old-timer" amendment to the "Hockey Abolition" Bill C–22 and its subsequent passage into law that year. (Montreal, by the way, won the Stanley Cup.)

Another bizarre footnote in history is that the initial government action of putting a surgeon general's stamp on pucks warning that excessive hockey can lead to divorce or death was found to be totally ineffective.

The Rules   In theory, players aren't allowed to check, crush, maim, or hack the opposition. They're also encouraged to avoid these same injuries to themselves. In practice this means each player is responsible for avoiding running into himself, another player, the boards, and the edge of the goal, and for avoiding a coronary at a face-off. (The rule disallowing slapshots was rescinded when it was found no Old-timer could lift his stick more than sixteen inches off the ice at any time without falling.)

The Future   The latest wrinkle in Old-timer hockey has four teams playing two separate games simultaneously across the ice. This approach was introduced once it was noticed that it took four Old-timers to make one real hockey player (i.e., If it takes only half as long to get tired, but twice as long to rest up, then any player is one-quarter as effective). The new approach is reportedly a great success.

More and more farmers are now playing Old-timer hockey in the winter instead of going someplace warm on holidays to fish or play in the water. They say the cold, the competition, and the coronaries serve as theoretical guidelines for the practice of farming.

◀ **thirty-four** ▶

The End of the Line

And so it goes. Theory dissolves into practice. Winter dissolves into spring. The seemingly endless cycle of farming continues.

That's farming in a nutshell.

I realize that to some this may appear to be farming in a nuthouse, but it's the difference between the theory of farming as seen by the outside world, and that practised by a farmer.

The outside world has a theoretical understanding of farming, but little knowledge of the reality of life down on the back 40.

This book illustrates what happens when the theory of farming is put into practice.

Whether seeding a crop, harvesting a crop, or weeping over a crop, my grain is always a headache.

About the Author

Aeneas Precht was born in North Battleford, Saskatchewan, in 1947. He grew up on a farm near Fielding, Saskatchewan. In 1969, he graduated from Simon Fraser University, British Columbia, and spent the next 10 years working and exploring Canada from sea to sea to sea. He began his writing career in Grand Falls, Newfoundland, as a reporter/feature writer for the Robinson–Blackmore chain of newspapers. He then returned to Fielding, where he now resides. He's an inveterate sailer and outdoorsman who spends his spare time and money on sailing, traveling, photography, sculpture, and inventions. He now makes his living as a writer, a broadcaster, a farmer, and a repairman of boats, trailers, and motorhomes. This is his first book.